RULES & TOOLS
FOR LEADERS

RULES & TOOLS
FOR LEADERS

*From Developing Your Own Skills
to Running Organizations of Any Size,
Practical Advice for Leaders at All Levels*

4TH EDITION

Perry M. Smith
Jeffrey W. Foley

A Perigee Book

A PERIGEE BOOK
Published by the Penguin Group
Penguin Group (USA) Inc.
375 Hudson Street, New York, New York 10014, USA

USA | Canada | UK | Ireland | Australia | New Zealand | India | South Africa | China

Penguin Books Ltd., Registered Offices: 80 Strand, London WC2R 0RL, England
For more information about the Penguin Group, visit penguin.com.

Revised Perigee trade paperback ISBN: 978-0-399-16351-7

The Library of Congress has cataloged the Avery edition as follows:

Smith. Perry M.
Rules & tools for leaders : how to run an organization successfully / by Perry M. Smith
p. cm.
Includes bibliographical references and index.
ISBN: 0-89529-835-X
1. Leadership.   2. Executives.   3. Management   4. Organization   I. Title.
HD57.7.S69   1998
658.4'092—dc21   98-17845 CIP

PUBLISHING HISTORY
Avery edition published 1998
First Perigee edition / July 2002
Revised Perigee trade paperback edition / August 2013

PRINTED IN THE UNITED STATES OF AMERICA

10   9   8

Most Perigee books are available at special quantity discounts for bulk purchases for
sales promotions, premiums, fund-raising, or educational use. Special books, or book excerpts,
can also be created to fit specific needs. For details, write: Special.Markets@us.penguingroup.com.

CONTENTS

FOREWORD

Running a large organization is challenging work. It also can be rewarding and uplifting. Good management, characterized by strong leadership based on sound judgment and integrity, is required in virtually any endeavor. Although there are many good books on management and leadership, what has been needed is a short, down-to-earth guide for busy leaders, to help them cope with the tougher issues. Perry Smith and Jeff Foley have written that guide, and leaders and associates alike can benefit from their ideas, insights, and rules of thumb.

Rules & Tools for Leaders is refreshing not only for its valuable content but also for the clarity of language and the crispness of the authors' writing style. They get to their points fast. This is a "tuned in" book. It deals with the real issues, legitimate dilemmas, and myriad possibilities that confront leaders. With extensive experience in running organizations, along with teaching and research in leadership and management, Smith and Foley have accomplished what many others would love to have done: They have written a guide that both leaders and associates can use to be more effective in their professional lives.

The original version of this book seemed to say essentially all that needed to be said about practicable leadership. But the demands on leaders continue to change. Current events in the business, government, and nongovernment organization sections have highlighted the importance of character and ethics in leadership and the importance of building teams whose members come from a wide variety of cultures. These considerations have been duly integrated into this book.

Although it deals with complex topics, there is a deceptive simplicity to this sophisticated volume. In one sense, it is the thoughtful reader's how-to book in the field of management. Those of us who have tried to learn plumbing or how to golf from a book know the limitations of the form. It is unrealistic to believe that anyone will become master of all he or she surveys in an executive suite as the result of one quick pass through *Rules & Tools for Leaders*. On the other hand, you have come to the right place if you are interested in a working visit with two talented, knowledgeable, and highly articulate executives who have many valuable perceptions to share. Most important, I believe you'll be inspired by Perry Smith and Jeff Foley to get your own creative juices flowing no matter what role you are playing in your organization. This is the kind of book that you will want to revisit periodically throughout your professional career.

Beyond the case studies and checklists, and the chapters ranging from strategic planning to personal introspection, *Rules & Tools for Leaders* has a deeper and wider application. We live in an era of unprecedented commercial, technological, and military challenge. We earn our daily bread in an increasingly competitive environment; markets have taken on truly global proportions. How well our nation manages its considerable assets—how effectively our government, industry, and other institutions utilize human, material, and financial resources—obviously are critical factors in determining our future prosperity. It is as simple, and yet as complex, as that.

Fortunately, management and leadership skills can be strengthened through learning. *Rules & Tools for Leaders* contributes to developing, honing, and refining these essential skills in a very specific way. The beneficiaries will be not only individual leaders and their organizations, but also, ultimately, the confederation that we call the free enterprise system.

For further information, as the old saying goes, inquire within.

—Norman R. Augustine
Retired Chairman and Chief Executive Officer,
Lockheed Martin Corporation,
Former Undersecretary, U.S. Army

PREFACE

For many years, Perry looked for a practical guide to running organizations. Since such a guidebook was nowhere to be found, he decided to write one himself. He did so while serving as the commandant of, and teaching executive leadership at, the National War College in Washington, DC—the senior professional school for career civilian and military officials with the highest potential for leadership. Jeff joined the writing team in 2011. Having recently retired from the Army, Jeff brought fresh ideas and insights. He wrote five new chapters and made dozens of suggestions for changes and updates.

It is our intention to provide a tool kit with many helpful rules of thumb and checklists not only for leaders but also for those who play supporting roles in organizations large and small. *Rules & Tools for Leaders* is a very personal yet universally applicable book in that it incorporates the many insights that we gained over more than thirty years of work in organizations in the United States and abroad.

We have spent much of the past thirty years teaching leadership to a wide variety of audiences. Our professional backgrounds have allowed us to bring leadership ideas from the military to corporate executives. In turn, we've been able to introduce the best of the leadership techniques developed by such visionary companies as Microsoft, UPS, Texas Instruments, Intel, Lockheed Martin, and Bridgestone to hospitals, foundations, associations, churches, manufacturing plants, government agencies, and military staff colleges.

Leaders count. People at the top can and should make a difference. Leaders influence what products are brought to market—the music we hear, the fashions we wear, the food we eat. They determine which neighborhoods will be wiped out by a new highway, which laws get passed, which initiatives get support. Leaders mold the daily performance—and ultimately an organization—by setting standards, by establishing and maintaining a network of communications, by nurturing relationships, and by motivating associates. Furthermore, leaders can affect permanently an organization by creating and implementing a strategic vision with specific long-term goals.

The future is not already determined. What will happen in the next twenty or thirty years will be, in large part, the consequence of decisions that influential leaders make within their organizations today. *Rules & Tools for Leaders* is the handbook for making those decisions in an organized, intelligent, ethical, and insightful manner.

We believe this book will help.

—Perry M. Smith
Jeffrey W. Foley

INTRODUCTION

> If you wish success in life, make perseverance your bosom friend, experience your wise counselor, caution your elder brother, and hope your guardian genius.
>
> —*Joseph Addison*

> A good leader inspires people to have confidence in the leader; a great leader inspires people to have confidence in themselves.
>
> —*Steve Jobs*

This is a very basic book to help managers, supervisors, and administrators to be better leaders. If you are looking for concepts, philosophies, paradigms, or academic treatises, this definitely is not the book for you. Put it back on the shelf now. But if you are looking for a handy, up-to-date tool kit and guidebook on leadership, you have come to the right place. This book will serve as a source of advice as you enhance your leadership skills and as a double check when you are making tough decisions for your organization.

Rules & Tools for Leaders was designed for those busy leaders and managers who might have a few hours on an airplane or on a quiet Sunday afternoon. This short book contains hundreds of helpful hints on dealing with the tough issues that lie ahead. The text is also designed for associates who must deal with their bosses and are interested in understanding the dilemmas that these leaders might be facing. In addition, it is structured for use in management and leadership courses, to augment the more theoretical works that are available in the literature.

From many years of experience, we learned that development as a leader is a transformational journey that begins with developing yourself as a leader, through leading others, to ultimately leading organizations. Learning to lead in each of these areas is a lifelong task. This new edition of *Rules & Tools for Leaders* includes new and revised content and is reorganized to make it even more accessible and valuable to the busy leader. We've divided the book into relevant parts with very specific chapter titles that will guide you to exactly where you want to go for the advice you'll need—when you need it.

We wrote this book to share our personal experiences with both failure and achievement. The setbacks provided the most valuable lessons, but we also gained knowledge and insight from some successful ventures. Our approach stems not only from our extensive military experience at West Point, out in the field, in combat, and at the Pentagon, but also from our work with several major organizations, including Duke Power, Tiffany and Company, Caterpillar, the Kellogg Foundation, *U.S. News & World Report*, the Goizueta Business School, NBC TV, Shaw Industries, the Bridgestone Tire Company, nonprofits, and universities. We have also been able to include insights from the many leaders with whom we have interacted in a wide range of endeavors.

We trust that this new edition of the book is that much better for what we have learned about leadership over the years since the first publication. Readers of earlier versions of this book often comment to us that what they like most is the straightforward language and the handy checklists, which we have retained.

Rules & Tools for Leaders is your tool kit for the future. We wrote it in the hope that it will not simply be read once, but be referred to time and time again. Use it well and use it often. Share it with your colleagues and employees. Let us know how we can improve it. Write to Perry at genpsmith@aol.com or to Jeff at jwfoley@icloud.com.

Good reading and good leading.

PART I

Developing Yourself
as a Leader

1

BECOMING SELF-AWARE

The Importance of Introspection

■ ■ ■

I worry about the self-made man who worships his maker.
—*Bishop Albert Stewart*

Picture yourself in a room of mirrors. Some mirrors give accurate reflections so that you can get a true picture of what you really look like. Some mirrors distort your image. The people around you—your employees, peers, and bosses—are like those mirrors. Even the most consistent leaders are viewed in different ways by many different people. While it is important to avoid becoming paranoid or defensive concerning misperceptions about you, you need to develop the self-awareness that you are projecting the right image. The value of that image is found in your willingness to listen, to accept criticism, to learn from mistakes, and to embody the many qualities that define an outstanding leader.

You are really five people in one: (1) who you think you are, (2) who your subordinates think you are, (3) who your peers think you are, and (4) who your bosses think you are. And then there's the last one, (5) the indefinable notion of who you *really* are. How others see you is often at odds with how you see yourself, for better or worse. Qualities, both positive and negative, may be overestimated or exaggerated. You are probably not as brilliant, decisive, communicative, or charismatic as you sometimes think you are.

Perceptions can be deceiving: Are you a chronic drinker because you've had a few too many on a rare occasion? Are you senile because you nodded off in the midst of a long, boring meeting? Are you heavy-fisted in demanding authority if you fire an associate? Are you shallow because you make a quick decision?

Mature leaders are aware of these "perception gaps." They work hard to become self-aware and to separate what's real from what's not, to get feedback, and to take corrective action when appropriate.

Perhaps the greatest benefit from objective introspection is improvement of your performance. Leaders who are self-aware, who recognize and maximize their strengths, and who understand and compensate for weaknesses perform much better than those who do not (or cannot) understand themselves. If fact, self-awareness combined with appropriate action can help avoid mistakes. Furthermore, an introspective leader builds an aura of self-confidence that engenders respect. Introspection is a process that can only be accomplished with systematic and regular attention. Seeking out the services of professionals or organizations, such as the Center for Creative Leadership in Greensboro, North Carolina, or the Gallup Leadership Institute, can be an invaluable investment.

Knowing yourself, your ideals, your psychological and spiritual strengths and weaknesses can improve your ability to provide enlightened leadership. It is healthful and useful to ask yourself questions such as:

"What values do I really hold dear?"

"What are my most deeply held prejudices?"

"Do I 'walk my talk'?"

"Do I really practice what I preach?"

Capable leaders need to have a realistic understanding of who they are in order to avoid becoming ineffective, arrogant, or irrelevant. Persistent self-evaluation involves assessing your on-the-job effectiveness—asking yourself the hard questions about what you do and how you do it.

The Hard Questions

Every performance evaluation asks for employers to rate their staff on a number of key issues, from productivity and job knowledge to working relationships and managerial skills. Periodic self-evaluation will help you evaluate those qualities, habits, and skills that you should expect in yourself and your associates.

Do You Enjoy Your Job?

By letting people know that you are enjoying your job, you can help create a healthy atmosphere in your organization. Leaders who enjoy their jobs, and show everyone they do, often help their associates enjoy their jobs as well. Smiles and good words are usually contagious. Do you feel genuine joy in the successes of your subordinates? Let them know when you are pleased with their work and that you look forward to the workday because you're playing on a good team.

How Do You Define Ambition?

Is your ambition focused on yourself or your associates and organization? Too many people who have moved to top positions in our businesses and government have been so personally ambitious that they have forgotten that their first responsibility is to the mission and goals of the country or organization. When ambition drives the needs of the organization, everyone will benefit and rewards will be greater in the long run. Part of being a good leader is realizing that you are there to provide a service to the people, not vice versa.

Are You an Optimist or a Pessimist?

If you are constantly optimistic, always wearing rose-colored glasses, you may lose the respect of associates because you are unable to acknowledge the weaker sides of your organization. Perhaps you refuse to see the tough problems. On the other hand, if you are constantly pessimistic and cynical, the organization's morale probably will suffer. A pragmatically optimistic individual who is not a starry-eyed dreamer, but who comes to work with a lot of enthusiasm and optimism, tends to be an effective and respected leader. Although a cynic might start out as a competent leader, cynicism and pessimism are likely to transfer negatively throughout the organization.

How Do Your Ethics and Values Have an Impact on Your Leadership?

Do you ever mention spiritual or moral values in your speeches or in your writings? Have you ever been asked to stand up in front of a religious group and give a talk? Many associates will observe whether you are committed to a system of ethics and values. They will hope for a leader who shares their values. You should be wary, however, about the danger of seeming to impose your standards on others. Leaders who are, or appear to be, self-righteous often fail to gain or maintain good rapport with a large number of employees.

Leaders must realize that personal integrity and institutional integrity meet in the front office. If you have a commitment to integrity—if you talk about it, write about it, mean it, and live it— there is a good chance that institutional and personal integrity throughout the organization will remain high. If, however, you do not concern yourself with it and are willing to allow the rules to be bent, institutional integrity may degenerate rapidly. As a leader, your concern with integrity will largely determine the standards and pride of the entire organization.

Do You Recognize the Consequences of Your "After Hours" Conduct?

Poor personal conduct has undone many a leader. What you do "after hours" is integral to your own success and that of your organization. You don't have to look far to see examples of how personal conduct—from substance abuse to questionable moral behavior—has led to the downfall of potentially great leaders.

Those who have psychological or health problems relating to alcohol or drug abuse often find their problems magnified. Ask yourself the hard questions: "Now that I'm a leader, what should be my approach to alcohol consumption?" "How are my drinking habits viewed by others?" The perception of alcoholism in a leader is often as damaging as the reality of alcoholism. Abuse of illegal drugs—or even prescription drugs—will have an equally deleterious effect that may result not only in your own failure to lead effectively but also in legal action against you.

Sexual misconduct seems rampant (or at least commands more than its share of media attention) and the consequences are clear. Moral issues aside, no matter what your field—business, government, military, or nonprofit—you are being scrutinized and judged. Even the perception of transgression can damage your own reputation and that of your organization. In this era of fast communication where every rumor and nuance can be transmitted globally in an instant, no one is immune from accusation or innuendo.

How Are You Perceived by Others?

Do people fear you, distrust you, like you, respect you, or love you? Are they comfortable with you or are they afraid of you? How people perceive you is important; if your coworkers feel good about you, respect and admire you, there will be better communication and enhanced productivity. Without this trust, others may withhold information for fear that you might overreact or make premature and unfounded judgments about them and their ideas. When you create an atmosphere of trust and confidence, your associates will feel free to be open and honest with you.

Are You Accessible?

What is your demeanor in the office? Do you sit behind your desk, using it as a shield or a sword? Or are you willing to step away from the seat of authority? Are you able, figuratively, to wrap your arms around people with warmth and concern? When discussing an issue with you, do associates feel that they can break through the interpersonal barriers that exist between subordinates and the boss? Many leaders are visible but not approachable and don't realize how their demeanor makes people reluctant to approach them.

A certain level of intensity comes with the role of leadership. But ask yourself what kind of attitude do you project as you enter a meeting, carry on a conversation, or make a speech. Are you able to convey just the right level of selfless concern, or do the burdens and responsibilities of leadership cause you to have an anxious air about you most of the time? Do you sit on the front edge of your chair? Do you constantly interrupt people when they are trying to tell you something? Awareness of these signals of impatience can help you evaluate whether your intensity adds to or detracts from your success as a leader.

Are You an Effective Communicator?

How well do you speak? Are your speeches and talks well crafted and to the point? Are your conversations meaningful and heartfelt? Do you look people in the eye when you are speaking to them? Are you able to break down the barriers between the ranks in order to communicate effectively yet with authority?

How well do you write? While speaking to groups or one-on-one is important, the permanence of the written word makes clear communication vital for leaders. From employee evaluations to emails, your skill—or lack of it—can make a tremendous impact on your organization and the people in it. Carelessly written emails can cause confusion—or even leave you and your organization vulnerable to lawsuits. (A wise manager once declared that after three email exchanges, if a problem is not resolved, get on the phone!) If performance appraisals are poorly written, you are doing a disservice to your associates. Position papers, reports, letters of recommendation, referrals, and even thank-you notes each play a vital role in the way you are perceived by everyone inside *and* outside your organization. Good communication takes maintenance work.

Let go of your ego and ask for help to edit your important communications. If you learn to write well, you can better serve your organization. Just as importantly your writing skills will be admired and appreciated. As John Kenneth Galbraith has written, "If you write well, you will automatically get attention."

Effective communication is a powerful means through which you can convince your associates that you are rightfully in a leadership role.

How Well Do You Listen?

Listening is an acquired art that requires self-discipline and well-developed communication skills. Leaders should listen and listen and listen; only through listening can you find out what's really going on. If an associate raises an issue and you do not allow the full case to be stated, you are likely to understand only a piece of the story and the problem probably will not be solved. In addition, the individual who raised the problem will be frustrated with the lack of opportunity to lay the whole issue on the table and to make sure you fully understand the situation.

There are two general kinds of listening. The first, passive listening, means that you listen without interruption: no comments or questions until the speaker has had a reasonable opportunity to express his or her views. The second, active listening, implies that you ask questions occasionally so that you confirm what is being said and that you have a clear understanding of the case. Each occasion may demand one or the other, but an effective leader is capable of doing both and will understand when to use passive or active listening. When in doubt, err on the side of passive rather than active listening.

Are You Open to Criticism and to the Truth?

Who tells you all the news—good and bad? It is important to have people who are close by who are honest and forthright, who give you the bad news as well as the good news, and who are not bootlickers or apple polishers. The best leaders foster a willingness in their associates to tell what they think and not what makes the boss happy. You need to periodically ask yourself: "Who around me is willing to tell the full story?"

Leaders who react emotionally or violently to criticism often fail as leaders because, over time, they lose touch with the most important and the most difficult issues. Their associates are afraid to criticize them. These leaders also tend to lose some of their best people who, out of frustration, move on to other places where constructive criticism is part of the organizational climate. Leaders who take criticism poorly damage vital feedback mechanisms and may cause associates to jump ship. When such leaders face crises, they will search in vain for the creative associates who could have bailed them out.

Equally important, over time, leaders who have the reputation of refusing to accept criticism or reacting inappropriately to it have difficulty recruiting talented individuals. Nobody wants to work for a jerk!

Like Ed Koch, the former mayor of New York City, you should be asking often, "How am I doing?" Be prepared for the answer—and to act on it as needed.

Are You Self-Confident or Self-Delusional?

If you are secure within yourself and are capable of accepting criticism well, you can serve as a mature leader in many different positions. If you are basically insecure and worry a great deal about your performance and abilities, you may have a more difficult task. In general, your sense of security should increase as your organization succeeds. Many initially insecure people can build their self-confidence over time and can become mature, successful leaders.

Are You Reliable?

Have you canceled out of a meeting, speech, ceremony, visit, or social engagement at the last minute more times that you care to remember? Have you failed to deliver on your promises to your employees, peers, or bosses? You'll be able to ramp up your reliability rating if you avoid over-scheduling yourself. You should say no to tasks and responsibilities that you are unable or unwilling to fulfill. You still have a job to do—and you know what it is. But it doesn't mean you have to be a slave to everyone else's desires.

For many years, we have been impressed by the reliability and character of Colin Powell. Whenever he agrees to do something, he does it. Whenever we write to him, we always get an answer, and usually within a few days. General Powell is part of Perry's integrity brain trust. He was very helpful when Perry was trying to decide about quitting CNN on a major issue of integrity. Many people have commented on Powell's charisma, self-confidence, and speaking style. His extraordinary negotiation skills, his ability to think and act strategically, his integrity, and his reliability put him at the top of our list of role models for leaders to emulate.

Are You Decisive or Are You a "Decision Ducker"?

A witty person once said that there are three types of people: those who make things happen, those who watch things happen, and those who wonder what happened. Heed the words of Johann Schiller: "He who considers too much will perform too little." Top leaders should follow the 60 percent rule—when you have about 60 percent of the information that you need to make a decision, you should make it. If you wait much longer to get more information, your decision may come too late. Be a leader who makes things happen.

Leaders who constantly duck decisions create atmospheres of indecision. Such a climate causes the organization to drift. Too often, decisions that should be made by the boss end up being made by lower-level associates without full coordination. If top-level decisions are always left to associates, consistency and coherency of policy will suffer, even though many of those decisions may be good. If you prefer to have subordinate associates make most of the decisions, at least ensure that there are general rules of policy and coordination that apply to all decision-making processes.

Are You Flexible?

Are you so rigid in your thinking and lifestyle that you are not open to new ideas? Conversely, are you flexible to a fault? Do you swing with the breeze? Where do you fit on the continuum between too much flexibility and not enough? You must use good judgment when it comes to being steadfast. Good leaders are not pushovers, nor are they tyrants. Through carefully observing and understanding the dynamics of the organization, you should be able to decipher how flexible you need to be. As is true with many issues, it is best to avoid extremes.

Are You an Innovator?

Are you someone who hangs on to the status quo? Are your decisions and actions dictated by policies that do not allow much flexibility? General Matthew Ridgway, the great combat leader of World War II and Korea, made a very telling point after he retired from the top military position in the U.S. Army: "My greatest contribution as chief of staff was nourishing the mavericks." Are you someone who is open to suggestions, ideas, new thoughts, new directions, and new concepts? On the other hand, are you someone who innovates too much and creates turmoil within the organization because you are constantly changing your mind about policies, personnel, and other organizational issues? Have you found the proper balance between continuity and creativity? Some situations need and accept innovative solutions. In other situations, innovation must be adopted slowly and incrementally to preserve the existing strength of the organization. To know the answer, you must know the culture and temper of the organization.

Are You Able to See the Big Picture?

Are you able to put the mission, goals, requirements, and responsibilities of the organization into a broader context? Are you able to explain how your business or organization fits into this greater framework? A leader who conceptualizes well is usually a good planner and an excellent teacher. It is important to provide a comprehensive "big picture" that explains the visions, goals, and priorities of the organization.

Do You—and Those Around You—Understand and Accept Your Priorities?

Have you codified what the most important things are for your organization and discussed them with your associates? Do you, in fact, follow your own priorities? There should be a close correlation between the priorities of the leader and those of the organization. If you establish an agenda for yourself and/or your organization that you are unwilling or unable to follow, your actions will become the source of cynical comment and diminished morale.

How Much Time Do You Spend on Each Distinct Aspect of Your Job?

How much time to you spend on the "front lines"—visiting the shop floor, the manufacturing or maintenance areas, in the field, or with other units or parts of the organization? Are you interacting with your employees, peers, and bosses outside of set meetings? Are you following the "four-hour" rule—that is, no more than four hours a day in your office will help you focus your time on what needs to be done at your desk and what can be accomplished outside your office. And, most important, spending time with the troops will help you to keep the "Big Picture" of your organization in mind with your firsthand observations and knowledge.

Are You Tuned In or Are You Out of Touch?

Leaders who isolate themselves in their offices or who don't have the ability to reach out and learn what's really happening soon get a reputation for being out of touch. What are the best means for staying tuned in? Are your antennae out all the time? Do you have good feedback mechanisms? A lot of problems develop when associates realize that their leaders are unfamiliar with or uninvolved in their work. Some will be tempted to take advantage of the fact that they are not being observed carefully. Others will feel neglected and underappreciated because their leader does not seem involved and interested.

Do You Know Your People?

How many people within a large organization should a leader know personally? A good general number is three hundred. Leaders should know well their key associates throughout the organization. Furthermore, an effective leader is familiar with the important informal leaders, especially in the various minority groups. If the leader knows more than three hundred employees, he or she may be spending too much time learning (and retaining) names and too little time focusing on the important issues. On the other hand, if the leader knows fewer than three hundred individuals, he or she may be losing touch with people who can provide valuable information, ideas, and insights.

Are You an Effective Delegator?

Many bosses who have an enormous amount of talent—and energy—run their entire organization from the front office. Unfortunately, they do not help associates develop into future leaders. Leaders who are willing to delegate authority are not only encouraging leadership at lower levels, but also giving people a great deal of psychological reward. If you are willing to delegate rather liberally but with discernment, you are probably creating a healthy organization. Your associates should be able to carry on effectively if you should become disabled, incapacitated, or replaced by a less competent individual. The top leader should empower associates so that they have full authority to make decisions on their own. Many leaders delegate conditionally when they should empower cautiously. A leader should not be so aggressive in the desire to delegate that he or she loses touch and becomes nothing more than a traffic cop. Over-delegation can lead to the "Balkanization" of an organization, where no one is in charge.

Are You a "Heat Shield" for Your Associates?

Everyone has a boss. And one of your roles as a leader is to accept guidance and criticism from above and act on it in a mature way. If you are constantly magnifying the pressure that comes from your superiors, putting more and more pressure on your associates as a result, you may be doing a disservice to organizational morale and to your mission. At times, a leader should deflect these pressures; at other times, a leader should let some of these pressures flow through the organization. A good rule of thumb is to be a "heat shield" for any guidance and direction from above that will cause serious and lasting morale problems. You may not be able to deflect all of the heat from the big boss, but you should deflect some of it.

Do You Command or Demand the Respect of Your Associates?

A good leader commands a healthy respect without making others feel inferior or resentful. Everyone respects a leader who is a fair disciplinarian, who does not punish—or fire someone—without careful consideration, and who sets standards that he or she also is willing to maintain and uphold.

When you take time to counsel associates, to advise them of their responsibilities before taking action, to be tough but fair, you serve your institution, and your employees, well.

If you are bored, tired, or looking forward to retirement, you should probably accelerate that decision; retire next month and let someone else take the reins! The fact that you worked long and hard to reach the top does not justify the attitude that the company owes you a number of years in *semi-retirement*. If you are burned out, admit it and take early retirement. It is much better to leave a year early, rather than a year or more too late.

If, after going through the exercise of self-analysis, you decide that leadership is not for you, it is best to begin to make preparations for other work. People who do not find leadership an uplifting and rewarding experience should not seek leadership jobs, and should not stay in them. Honest introspection can help you decide whether you can march enthusiastically to the beat of the leadership drum.

Introspection Checklist

Introspection is a vital part of leadership. Leaders who know who they are and who recognize and use their strengths while understanding and compensating for their weaknesses, have a tremendous advantage. They perform much better than leaders who cannot or do not analyze and evaluate themselves. Asking yourself the following questions will not only serve as a reminder of the content of this chapter but allow you an opportunity to reflect again on the truly important things in your life and work:

☐ Do I enjoy my job?

☐ Am I ambitious, not only for myself but for others and for the organization?

☐ Do I see the glass half-empty or half-full?

☐ How do my ethics and values inform my leadership?

☐ Where do I rate on the integrity scale?

☐ Do I understand how my personal conduct has a positive or negative impact on my work?

☐ Are there "perception gaps" between how I see myself and how others see me?

☐ Does the attitude I project make me appear accessible or formidable?

☐ Do I speak and write clearly and persuasively?

☐ How well do I really listen?

☐ Am I open to criticism—and to the truth?

☐ Can people count on me—for support, for guidance—and even just to show up?

☐ Am I decisive or am I a "decision-ducker"?

☐ Can I adapt to change without falling for every faddish business theory that comes along?

☐ Have I found the middle ground between innovation and tradition?

☐ Do I miss the forest for the trees?

☐ Have I established—and do I follow—organizational priorities? And do my associates understand and follow them, too?

☐ Am I "tuned it" or out of touch?

☐ Do I delegate effectively without absolving myself of personal accountability?

☐ How well do I protect my people from pressure from above yet instill in them the appropriate level of urgency?

☐ Am I always learning—and encouraging and enabling others to do the same?

While these questions may certainly lead you to a degree of self-awareness, there are some personality assessment tools that may help you understand yourself better, such as the Myers-Briggs Type Indicator, the DiSC Assessment (Dominance, Influence, Steadiness, Conscientiousness), or other 360 assessment tools. In addition, an excellent book that can help you discover your strengths is *Now, Discover Your Strengths* by Marcus Buckingham and Donald O. Clifton.

2

BECOMING A LEADER OF CHARACTER

Integrity and More

■ ■ ■

> To be an effective strategic leader, you must have character
> and strategy . . . and if you must do without one, do without
> strategy.
>
> —*General Norman Schwarzkopf*

> I have a dream that my four little children will one day live in
> a nation where they will not be judged by the color of their
> skin, but by the content of their character.
>
> —*Martin Luther King Jr.*

Arguably the most important element of being a successful leader is being a person of character. Character represents the sum total of who we are as individuals—what is in our hearts and souls. Character serves as the foundation for our behavior, how we live our lives, the environment we create for our homes and places of work, and how we interact with others.

Unlike the leadership skills we see in others, evidenced through their behavior, character cannot be seen by simple observation. It takes concerted effort over time to demonstrate that you understand it.

Character and You

Being a leader of character is a lifelong process. While character begins taking shape in our youth with the influence of parents, siblings, relatives, teachers, coaches, religious leaders, and others within our immediate circle, as we age the sphere of influence expands to include our adult friends, spouses, children, bosses, colleagues, elected officials, historical figures, and so on.

There is no simple definition of "character." It is, according to one dictionary, the complex of mental and ethical traits marking and often individualizing a person. It comprises many aspects and is manifested in many ways.

Leaders of character:

- Have the moral courage to stand up for causes they believe in.

- Exhibit behavior that enables others to trust them, for they know that without trust, the team will fail.

- Follow a code of ethics—those rules of conduct that everyone is expected to obey.

- Display a passion for doing what is right.

- Possess the inner strength to solicit and accept feedback to improve themselves.

- Are not afraid to admit mistakes.

- Have the courage to hold themselves accountable for failures in their organization.

- Demonstrate true humility.

- Show tough love when the situation calls for it.

- Speak from the heart.

- Are kind, respectful, empathic, and compassionate.

- Are honest with their people.

- Keep their promises.

- Commit themselves with a profound sincerity to do their very best.

- Are selfless in their service to others.

- Understand the importance of the mission, but exercise the patience that gives others time to learn how to accomplish it.

- Walk the talk.

This is a tall order for anyone, but striving for what is most meaningful and important in your work and your life should be your priority.

"One of the finest soldiers to have ever served in our Army was Command Sergeant Major Thomas J. Clark, who exuded character in everything he said and did," recollects Jeff. "I will never forget the day Tom demonstrated so many of the character traits we seek in our leaders. During the military funeral of a soldier killed in Iraq that Tom and I were presiding over, the soldier's older brother became distraught and vocal in expressing all of those emotions that loved ones feel at times like this. Tom, who had seen a lot of deaths in war and knew the emotional trauma suffered by the families, saw a bad situation developing. Where most people would be unsure as to what to do, Tom had the confidence, courage, and compassion to act. He embraced the grieving brother, quietly consoling him throughout the service. Tom helped this brother, the family, and all those present to witness the honoring of this hero during a profound and dignified funeral ceremony."

Babe Didrikson Zaharias, who was a great athlete in the 1932 Olympics, later became a successful professional golfer. While playing in a professional tournament, she realized that she had somehow played the wrong golf ball when she hit her ball out of the rough. When the round was over, she appropriately penalized herself two strokes, which cost her first place in the tournament. Later, in a quiet conversation, one of her friends asked her, "Babe, why did you do that? No one would have known that you used the wrong ball." Babe answered, "Don't you understand? I would have known."

Didrikson Zaharias demonstrated the kind of personal integrity she derived from a set of principles developed not only from the influencers in her life, but from her life experiences. Her code ultimately guided her behavior, just as every leader's code should guide him or her—and every organization's code should guide it.

If character is the sum of our personal mental and personal traits, integrity is core of character. Or, as author Stephen Carter suggests, it is "first among virtues that define good character." Integrity implies not only wholeness but a firm adherence to a code of moral values and ethics that encompasses uprightness, honesty, truthfulness, candidness, faithfulness, justness, fairness, and, ultimately, trust.

In his bestselling book *The Five Dysfunctions of a Team*, Patrick Lencioni claims that the "lack of trust" is the most critical factor causing failure of a team. Trust is a factor in everything you do: the grocery store you patronize, restaurants you frequent, the religious institution you attend, the car dealership you shop at, the contractor you hire for your remodeling job. The element of trust is everywhere and we rely on it every day to guide our decisions.

The seeds of distrust are planted if others do not see you as a leader committed to living up to the standards established for all. Therefore, early in your tenure, you should look for opportunities to demonstrate your commitment to integrity. To earn trust is a significant and profound task. To keep it once you have earned it is equally important. Once trust is lost, it may never be regained.

Strong leaders need to be prepared to say no when ethics demand it. Ethical decisions become ever more complex as individuals grow in power, prestige, and rank. Loyalty and good moral values will sometimes be in conflict. To apply ethics with wisdom and maturity may be the greatest challenge—and the greatest opportunity—for the enlightened leader.

People of character and integrity seek to improve themselves as they move to higher and higher positions of responsibility. Unfortunately, all too frequently, the opposite occurs. As individuals climb up the slippery pole to success, they may "sell their souls" incrementally, making small compromises to their personal integrity in order to serve their ambitions or their egos. Junior executives who say to themselves, "I will never be like my dishonest or manipulative boss when I reach the top" too often find themselves eventually acting very much like that boss they once looked upon with disdain.

Scandals abound in businesses large and small, religious organizations, educational institutions, sports, and government. From Wall Street to Congress to the White House the cost of low integrity to individuals, to their firms, and to the institutions they represent can be staggering. The importance of ethics in private business may not be as obvious or as immediately pressing as the importance of ethics in government, but it is not an inconsequential factor in the long-term health of free enterprise systems throughout the world.

> **Labor to keep alive in your breast that little spark of
> celestial fire called conscience.**
> —George Washington

Being a leader of character is not negotiable—it is that simple.

Character and Your Organization

While integrity may begin with you, your organization must be built and operate on a strong ethical foundation.

A lack of institutional character will damage the credibility of the organization just as dramatically it does your own.

To be a leader of character you have to be an absolute believer in the values the organization espouses, whether they are codified in a mission statement, rules of conduct, published policies and procedures, or a credo. Every decision you make and every action you take will be dependent on adherence to these values.

To be most effective these values must be well known, well documented, and well marketed throughout the organization.

You should be looking constantly for opportunities to demonstrate your commitment to the organization's values. You should make values the subject of discussion at staff meetings, informal gatherings, during speeches, and at award and recognition ceremonies. Leaders of character also look for opportunities to share stories about employees who demonstrated behaviors based on the values that showed positive results for the organization. Because, aside from assuring that your own behavior is beyond reproach and that you broadcast your organization's values widely, your responsibility also includes developing others to become leaders of character. This is accomplished through leader development programs, individual mentorship programs, and counseling.

When you evaluate the moral dimensions of your organization's mission, know that it must ultimately be based on individual worth, human equality, and human dignity. You cannot afford to ignore these values in daily practice.

Integrity is not something that can be put on and taken off as we go to and from work. People who have demonstrated poor ethical behavior in their personal lives are less likely to become leaders of character. An individual who cheats on income tax forms, engages in spousal or child abuse, or even cheats at golf is also likely to violate standards of institutional integrity. When such people are placed in leadership positions, they can do serious damage to the organization or the institution, if not in the short-term then certainly over time.

To uphold the integrity of an organization requires diligence and attention. Leaders should be aware of the signs that people are falling short on the integrity meter, which may be evident when people knowingly make decisions that are inconsistent with the values of the organization, are not open to feedback, always look for easy solutions, never seek advice, conveniently forget agreements, are afraid to admit mistakes, lack compassion and respect for others, and are too quick to accept praise. A watchful eye will pay dividends.

Effective leaders take prompt corrective action when there are violations of integrity and, over time, upgrade the standards of institutional ethics and ensure that everybody understands their fundamental commitment to the values of the organization.

Integrity Checklist

Within an organization, there are certain areas and processes that especially challenge integrity. It is important for you to check periodically the following systems and procedures to ensure that high standards of integrity are being maintained:

☐ Management and business practices

☐ Customer solicitations

☐ Vendor relations

☐ Accounting

☐ Submission and implementation of budgets and programs

☐ Quality and inventory controls

☐ Hiring and termination policies

☐ Personnel training and testing

☐ Personnel records

☐ Recognition/Awards/Bonuses/Promotions

☐ Expense accounts

☐ Perquisites (perks)

☐ Diversity

☐ Equal employment opportunity programs

☐ Reporting lines

FOR FURTHER READING

The Power of Ethical Management by Kenneth Blanchard and Norman Vincent Peale

The Nightingale's Song by Robert Timberg

Integrity by Stephen L. Carter

John Adams by David McCullough

How Good People Make Tough Choices by Rushworth M. Kidder

3

LEARNING SELF-DISCIPLINE
Taking Control of Your Time and Your Calendar

■ ■ ■

Time is free, but it's priceless. You can't own it, but you can use it. You can't keep it, but you can spend it. Once you've lost it you can never get it back.

—*Harvey Mackay*

Don't say you don't have enough time. You have exactly the same number of hours per day that were given to Helen Keller, Pasteur, Michelangelo, Mother Teresa, Leonardo da Vinci, Thomas Jefferson, and Albert Einstein.

—*H. Jackson Brown Jr.*

There has been much research on the issue of time management for executives, leaders, and supervisors. We have had the opportunity to survey that research. In addition, we have had a chance to observe, at close hand, how leaders in corporations, nonprofits, government, and the military manage their time. Here are a few insights.

A CEO of a research firm that does technical work for large companies and for the government shared his insights on time management. He requests that meetings begin at 11 a.m., rather than 8, 9, or 10 a.m. He knows that many people have luncheon engagements and, hence, will get to the important issues quickly. When he chairs a meeting himself, this CEO follows a set pattern, allowing a maximum of one hour for the meeting. He always announces the purpose of the meeting at the start. If the purpose of the meeting is to reach a decision, he will often say, "In about forty minutes, I am going to ask for your views on a decision concerning the matter at hand." Also, those who do not speak up in a meeting usually are not invited back to the next meeting on the same subject. He feels that, if after an hour of discussion, certain individuals who have nothing at all to contribute will probably be wasting their time and company time at future meetings. This means that there will be a smaller group in attendance at the next meeting. That is okay since smaller groups are generally better at reaching decisions.

Although there is a danger of establishing a climate for "group-think" with this approach, this CEO has found a way to avoid the problem; he always ensures that there are one or two strong "devil's advocates" present at all decision meetings. He expects these people to challenge him with both criticism and alternative solutions to the problems at hand. Another time-management technique that this CEO uses is to time the length of his telephone calls. Any associate who speaks to him on the telephone for more than fifteen minutes on more than two occasions is counseled quietly about being too long-winded.

One of the most useful ways that Jeff has found to help use time effectively and efficiently is through the use of Stephen R. Covey's Urgent/Importance Matrix described in his book *The 7 Habits of Highly Effective People*. In determining how to put first things first (Habit #3), Covey contends that it is important to recognize the four distinct categories of tasks: (1) Important & Urgent; (2) Important & Not Urgent; (3) Urgent & Not Important; and (4) Not Urgent & Not Important. Thinking about priorities through the lens of this matrix can help you stay focused on what is important and reduce the time spent on less important matters or on managing crises.

Dwight D. Eisenhower, who had considerable leadership experience in the military, in international organizations, and in academia prior to his presidency, had a wonderful sense about where and how decisions should be made. He knew the difference between line and staff activities. He disciplined his in-box by sending numerous decision papers back to the appropriate cabinet or agency head. Ike would attach short notes to these papers indicating that this particular issue was not a presidential decision. He wanted and expected the respective sender to make the decision. Because he did so, Eisenhower had more time for the truly important or particularly sensitive issues, and for reflection and planning.

There are many useful time-management skills that you can develop as you move up the ladder. For example, an effective leader knows how to dictate clearly. Teddy Roosevelt was able to dictate more than twenty-five letters per hour. (He would alternate back and forth between two secretaries.) He was able to complete most of a full day's work of correspondence in a couple of hours through this dictation method. In the past, fast and efficient dictation required a secretary who took dictation well. However, voice recognition software is now available, so that leaders can talk directly to their computers. Hence, dictation, once a dying art, has made a significant comeback. Perry learned from Roosevelt and wrote most of his books by using the dictation method. This method tends to lead to short sentences without many long phrases or fancy words. In turn, the books make for easy reading.

Another aspect of managing time is speed-reading. Time can be better utilized if a leader can read very fast and rapidly find the essence of issues. A speed-reading course, or just practicing your reading, is very helpful. In addition, there is speed-reading software available for those leaders who use computers and email extensively. (Speed Reader-X is highly recommended.) If you can get through an in-box in an hour or two (whereas it might take slower readers half a day or more), you will have more time to be out with your people, to have substantive meetings on important issues, and to be a true leader, rather than just a desk manager.

You should work carefully to design a weekly and monthly schedule that fits your time clock, your body rhythms, and your priorities.

Maintaining "open time" every day is a helpful idea. This time should be set aside for thinking, handling crises, seeing unexpected visitors, or dealing with fast-moving issues.

If commitments fill your calendar at fifteen- or thirty-minute intervals from morning to night, you are managing your time poorly. You probably are getting into too much detail and not allowing yourself to think and plan. Moreover, associates who really need to see you on short notice may not be able to reach you promptly because your calendar is completely full.

As a general rule, you should not schedule more than one event per hour. Furthermore, your schedule should allow open time between meetings and events. Use this time to return phone calls, to work on items in your in-box, and to prepare for the next commitment. It is a reality that as you receive promotions, there will be increasing demands on your time. More and more people will want and need to see you. Work smarter, not harder; learn to say no to time-wasters. Thus you will be able to deal more efficiently with information overload. The key is to understand that as the leader, you have the authority to manage your time. However, time management takes work, a disciplined office, a tough-minded attitude, and good planning.

Meeting Checklist

This checklist is designed to improve the effectiveness of the meeting environment, by focusing on the key elements of any meeting, from attendees to the agenda to the time allocated.

☐ What is the purpose of the meeting?

☐ What is the agenda?

☐ Who will be in attendance?

☐ Have invitations been sent to all the corporate divisions, regional offices, international bureaus, factories, sales offices, etc.?

☐ Will a lawyer be in attendance?

☐ Will a public affairs person be in attendance?

☐ If key players cannot attend, can they be hooked up through a conference call, a teleconference system, or some other means?

☐ Do I intend to run the meeting myself or to allow someone else to chair the meeting?

☐ Do I have an overall policy on length of meetings, number of presentations, and length of presentations?

☐ In this meeting, do I intend to hold to these constraints?

☐ If not, do I intend to announce my position at the start of the meeting?

☐ How much time is allocated for the meeting?

☐ What is the start time and the end time?

☐ Have I announced the start and end times of the meeting ahead of time?

☐ Do any key players have to leave early? If so, who? Should the agenda be adjusted accordingly to give them a time to speak before they must leave?

☐ Are there presentations to be made?

☐ If so, by whom?

☐ Is there a time limit placed on each presentation?

☐ Will there be enough time for adequate discussion?

☐ What is my meeting strategy?

☐ What is my plan for keeping the meeting on track?

☐ Who are the main antagonists?

☐ Is compromise possible?

☐ Is compromise wise? Will it lead to a watered-down solution?

☐ Will decisions be made during the meeting?

☐ If so, will I announce them at the end?

☐ If not, should I announce when and how the decisions will be made?

☐ Who will be responsible for the implementation of the decisions?

☐ Who will be the recorder for the meeting?

☐ Will there be minutes?

☐ Will action items be committed to writing after the meeting?

☐ Will additional meetings be needed?

☐ Should these meetings be announced prior to the end of this meeting?

☐ If not, will I announce that this is the final meeting on the subject?

MANAGING THE ELECTRONIC WORLD

The Latest Challenge to Today's Leaders

■ ■ ■

Many people feel they must multitask because everybody else is multitasking, but this is partly because they are all interrupting each other so much.

—*Marilyn vos Savant*

As we all know, cell phones, smart devices, and computers have provided us access to an immense amount of information, which is readily available for our every need. There is no doubt that these devices have made us more efficient and increased productivity, but at what price? Parents reading work-related emails at their children's weekend sporting events, friends taking calls during dinner with each other, attendees working their smartphones during a briefing. All of these events happen every day, but the excuse given is "I know I shouldn't do it, but I have to answer right away." Although there are many cases when people must be immediately accessible, for most of us, is that really true? In many cases, if that email from Corporate goes unanswered for a few hours, the company is not going to go bankrupt, and if that call from the boss goes to voice mail, he or she will not be upset if you call back a little later. Do you allow your electronic devices to run your life or do you allow them to assist you to manage your time to gain better work-life balance?

Leadership is all about people and the best way to lead is through personal, face-to-face contact. While computers, cell phones, and other smart devices allow leaders to be immediately accessible and readily informed, personal contact with your subordinates is vital to effective leadership. Eye contact with a subordinate not only ensures that any message given is understood; it also allows the subordinate to ask questions and prevents frustration while waiting for an electronic response.

Email and texting can be, if used correctly, powerful tools for communicating within an organization. Caution must be considered, however, as these same forms of communication can also be very detrimental to the organization. Be very careful how you respond to emails that make you angry. Email confrontations usually turn hateful, create unnecessary anxiety and stress, and ultimately adversely impact important relationships between people and organizations. Think hard before you enter into an email confrontation. Consider calling or meeting with the person. You should never reprimand or scold anyone using email. Misuse of email or texting as a means of communicating with people can become a powerful team destroyer.

Effective leaders use their electronic devices to enhance their leadership style, not as a replacement for personal contact with those they lead. Effective management of your electronic devices should allow you more time to interact with your subordinates, think strategically about how to better support your organization and its overall mission, and develop a better work-life balance. Your son's home run in the bottom of the ninth to win the Little League game, your daughter's role of Wendy in *Peter Pan*, and that special anniversary will only happen once. Do you really want to miss them because of an email or a routine phone call? Effective leaders do not allow their electronic devices to control their lives.

Years ago, when we first started using electronic devices, whether they were pagers, PDAs, computers, or cell phones, we were told that they would make our lives more manageable. These devices would make us more efficient and therefore allow us more "free time" to spend on the things we really desired to do. Oh, how wrong were the experts! Today, the vast majority of leaders are completely attached to their electronic devices through smartphones and wireless connections. On most evenings, leaders are doing significant amounts of work through the use of email correspondence at home. In order for leaders to effectively lead their people, they must properly manage their time. In his book *How to Get Control of Your Time and Your Life*, Alan Lakein says "Time = life; therefore, waste your time and waste your life, or master your time and master your life." Managing your electronic workspace is vital to improving your leadership skills. Managing your time properly will allow you greater opportunities to interact with your team.

Smartphones provide one of today's top management challenges. The convenience and mobility of these devices allow leaders to be more accessible and efficient. However, if not managed properly, these attributes can also be detrimental. In an era when smartphones allow leaders to be constantly connected to their superiors, they often feel compelled to answer every question from the boss, as soon as it is asked. They may be both disregarding and alienating the best resources they have to answer the question: the members of their team. Too often, smartphones force us into providing inaccurate information because we haven't taken the time to consult with those who may have a more complete answer to the question. This starts an inevitable "circular dialogue" where one answer prompts the requester to ask another clarification question, which prompts another, and another. If time had been taken to think the original question through, a complete answer could have been given the first time. Time is wasted while each party waits for the other's phone call.

The computer is the other culprit that can consume your time and detract from your ability to adequately lead your team. Whether it is a desktop, laptop, tablet, or notebook, the device that we count on for most of our daily information can consume our lives. Constantly waiting for that one email from our boss that we believe must be responded to immediately can cause us to miss our daughter's game-winning goal or our son's recital. Because information is so readily available, computers and other devices encourage micromanagement. They often stifle an atmosphere of empowerment, trust, and mentorship. The overuse of these devices encourages constant crisis management because it stifles discussion and promotes quick action as soon as the email is received. Computers and other devices allow leaders to communicate tough decisions while often avoiding, in the short term, the negative feedback caused by their decisions. To paraphrase Robin Williams as the Genie in the Walt Disney remake of *Aladdin*, "Immense power, in a little teeny space!"

Taking Charge

The first thing we can do to gain control of our electronic devices is probably the simplest: TURN THEM OFF! We can do this physically by the on/off switch or by using the multitude of options contained in the devices. Simply muting the cell phone will keep you focused on the conversation at hand. You should take steps to prevent the distracting buzz or ring. Also, when you are in your office having a discussion with visitors or associates, shut down the email notification sounds and turn off your screen. Something as simple as turning the screen away so neither of you can see it is also effective to avoid distractions. Make a conscious decision to place your smart device in a location where you cannot access it until your meeting is complete.

Another method used by senior people is as follows: Prior to a meeting, give your device to a trusted subordinate who will not be in the meeting room and have that person screen your calls. Give your assistant one or two levels of priority for calls. The assistant can provide a quick response to each caller, such as "The boss is in a meeting and will get back to you after it concludes" or, when vital issues are involved, your assistant can interrupt the meeting to get you the message.

You can also control how you handle the information that flows into your devices by "batching" activities. Select a period of time and complete all *like* tasks during that period. For example, complete all email activities in a sixty-minute period once or twice a day. During that time frame you only respond to emails. You accept no phone calls and attend no meetings. When you reach the end of the sixty minutes, you stop your email activities and move to a different pursuit. Completing like activities all at one time allows you to put your full concentration and effort into a single task. This will reduce the distractions that multitasking creates.

There are those of us who have a fear of turning off our devices, because we believe we must be immediately accessible to our associates and our superiors. Don't assume that you are the only person who has answers to their questions. While in some cases this assumption may be true, in most cases others can provide answers just a well. You must train your subordinates to handle the delegated authority. You must clearly articulate any desired outcome. Any constraints or boundaries must be clearly communicated and you must be available to answer any questions or provide additional advice. Proper delegation in an organization breeds trust. Effective delegation produces a higher quality of work in an organization, greater motivation and sense of ownership in the workforce, and more time for you to focus on managerial and personal tasks. Proper delegation and empowerment allows all of us to gain better control of both our lives and our electronic devices.

In order to reduce the number of voice mails, emails, and text messages you receive on your devices while you're away from the office, designate someone on your team to make decisions in your stead. Obviously, a number of issues will arise that require your personal attention, but determine which things can be handled by subordinates and allow them the authority to handle them. Most important, when subordinates contact you too often via an electronic device, give them strong guidance on the need to exercise self-discipline and electronic restraint.

When you are on vacation, designate an assistant to respond to any inquiries. This will reduce the number of messages you receive, cultivate a trusting relationship with your assistant, and provide him or her experience with making difficult decisions.

Attempting to lead your team through your computer is another major mistake many leaders make. In order to more efficiently gain control of your email, use the four Ds:

1. Do It

The first decision you should make once you receive an email is "Do I need to take an action or can someone else complete the action?" If you decide that it is your action to take, attempt to only touch that email once. This will help you reduce the number of emails in your mailbox and allow you to concentrate on those that are truly important: If someone else can complete the action . . .

2. Delegate It

If you delegate an email, be sure to inform the delegate what you need done and who is due the response. If you decide that you need to take the action, then . . .

3. Designate It

By designating it, you assign time in your schedule to complete the action or task. If you decide that there is no action required by you or any other member of your team, and you don't need to save this information for future use . . .

4. Delete It

There are many other techniques available to help you organize your electronic world, many of which are included in the email applications that are included in your electronic device. If you color-code incoming emails based on your personal priorities, you will immediately see important emails and work on the most important issues first. When you are away from the office, set incoming message rules that will automatically direct administrative emails to the proper subordinate. While you are on vacation, set a rule that will automatically forward messages from important seniors directly to your deputy or assistant, so he or she can expeditiously answer them without you having to get involved. Organize a set of folders by project to maintain an archive of important correspondence so you can remove emails from your mailbox yet still have immediate access if needed. Use the subject line to indicate whatever action you expect and request the same from associates. If you desire a result from an action you've delegated, use the "follow up" flag function. This approach will help remind you that you've asked for some action to be completed by a certain date. It will also indicate to the person you sent the email to that you are expecting some action by that date. The better organized your electronic mailbox, the more time you will have to meet, counsel, and mentor your subordinates.

Another way your computer can help you make better use of your time is if you effectively use the calendar application. Maintaining a complete and up-to-date calendar will not only manage your time better but will also help your subordinates. First and foremost, make your calendar available to your direct subordinates and, if feasible, to your entire team. This will help build trust within the team. It will also allow your subordinates to know when you may be available to discuss issues of importance, and it will reduce the number of interruptions when you are working on important tasks. Just as you do in email, use colors in your electronic calendar to categorize your appointments. This not only allows your team to know the types of issues you are working on, but also the colors are visually effective. Make sure you put all appointments (both personal and job-related) on this calendar. By doing so, you will allow your team to plan around your schedule. This is a good way to let your team know that a work-and-life balance is important to you and should be for them.

The key to leading your team in an electronic workplace is establishing your expectations and communicating them to your subordinates. If you want your subordinates to take the initiative and handle issues without having to ask you for direction, make sure they understand what you want, when you want it, and how you want it.

We have seen far too many senior leaders cause the lives of those they serve to suffer by abusing evening and weekend time—family time—with emails and phone calls for tasks that have no urgency at all. The consequences of this infringement of an employee's sacred off-duty time breeds dissention, distrust, and morale issues not just with the employee but with the family as well. The performance level of the organization—and ultimately the results the organization achieves—will suffer when this environment exists.

Good leaders establish a policy regarding how email and after-hours communications is to be handled and communicate that policy to the entire team. Good leaders ensure that off-duty engagement is for real urgent matters only. Whatever policy you establish, be relentless in its enforcement.

Checklist for Managing Your Electronic Devices

☐ TURN THEM OFF!

☐ Batch your activities.

☐ Delegate as much as possible: Responsibility cannot be delegated but authority can be.

☐ In dealing with electronic communications use the 4 Ds: Do It. Delegate It. Designate It. Delete It.

☐ Use installed applications to organize your electronic mailbox and calendar.

☐ Establish your expectations concerning electronic communications and explain them to your associates.

5

WORKING FOR THE BOSS

The Trials and Opportunities of Subordinates

■ ■ ■

Wars may be fought with weapons, but they are won by men. It is the spirit of the men who follow and of the man who leads that gains the victory.

—*George S. Patton*

All bosses have a boss.

—*Anonymous*

What is the best way to get your boss to be a better and more enlightened leader without endangering your relationship with him or her or putting your career at risk? Most senior leaders feel that they have already demonstrated their ability to lead. They rarely read management or leadership books and certainly don't think they need advice on leadership from their associates. Many bosses would be insulted if an associate gave them a book on leadership, for there would be an implied message that they needed help in this area.

One approach to dealing with weak or flawed bosses is to develop specific helping techniques. By making an effort to help, you will gain the respect and affection of your colleagues and you might be able to make a difference. One of the best ways to help bosses is to approach them at a social gathering or at a sports event, when they are relaxed and open to ideas. Start the conversation with something like "The folks on the line are pretty down in the dumps," or "We may need to do something to improve the morale of our employees." If you use this kind of an opening, it is helpful to have data that can demonstrate that there is, in fact, a problem of some kind. Such data might include unusually high absentee rates, an increase in the number of written complaints, negative feedback from union leaders, or a higher-than-normal rejection rate on the production line. If the boss picks up on your point, you might be able to make suggestions that will improve the situation and enhance his or her credibility.

Over time, as the boss gets used to your insights, you may be able to show him or her that some past decisions were faulty and need to be reworked. There are, of course, some risks in trying to guide your boss. Some bad bosses are not only reluctant to receive advice and criticism, but also vindictive. (Leaders who are reading this chapter might ask themselves, with as much objective introspection as they can muster, if they are receptive to criticism about their leadership.)

Another approach that may be effective is to suggest to the big boss that a subordinate leader be given an opportunity to attend a first-rate leadership program and to report back to the senior corporate officers on the insights that he or she gained from this experience. A better, but somewhat more risky approach is to suggest that the leader attend one of the weeklong programs at the Center for Creative Leadership at Greensboro, North Carolina, or the four-week courses held at many of the better business schools.

If you have to work for a weak boss, it may be helpful to think in terms of categories of bosses. Working for a wimp is different than working for a type A boss, a power-seeker, a laissez-faire individual, a mother hen, a big ego, or a country club boss. In the past forty years, both of us have either worked for or observed at close hand each type of boss described below:

Type A bosses are those who tend to micromanage, may be workaholics, and may demand that employees work excessively long hours. They often overreact to criticism and refuse to delegate. Subordinates should try to reason with type A bosses about unrealistic deadlines, for instance. If this doesn't work, standing up to them with firmness on a particularly unreasonable request often will get their attention and support: "I can get you an answer by the end of the day, but it will be garbage. How about giving me a week and I'll come up with something that we can all be proud of."

Power-seekers love to grab pieces of the action from parts of the organization that they do not control. "Turf" is terribly important to them, and they almost never give anything up, for fear that their power base may be diminished. Power-seekers tend to love self-designed reorganizations that normally lead to more people, bigger budgets, and more centralization. Employees learn to treat power-seekers with great care, but at times subordinates can effect changes by demonstrating that delegation and empowerment will cause workers to work harder and more efficiently, and therefore enhance the power-seeker's prestige. Subordinate leaders should explain with care that not only are the activities of the power-seeker causing morale problems throughout the workforce, but continuation of these activities may cause some of the more productive people to leave the firm or complain loudly to the power-seeker's big boss. Leaders on "power trips" tend to be personally insecure. Sometimes subordinates can play on these insecurities to help the power-seekers curb their worst traits.

Wimpy bosses tend to be indecisive and afraid to take strong action in any direction. Their philosophy of leadership seems to be "no runs, no hits, and no errors." For example, a wimpy boss would prefer to limp along with a weak associate rather than to fire that individual. As a subordinate associate, you can help a wimpy boss by making decisions for him or her and keeping your boss informed of the decisions that you have already made. If things go wrong, you volunteer to take the blame. You may not get credit for the successes, but at least the organization will not be paralyzed. One technique is to send indecisive bosses notes informing them about an action you are about to take and suggesting that if you do not hear from them within a week, you will press on. You should let the boss know that you are willing to take full responsibility for your action, in order to ease his or her mind.

Laissez-faire bosses are usually good ones to work for, in that they leave you alone and allow you to make decisions on your own. However, such a boss can become too far removed from the action. If this occurs, try to keep him or her informed regarding important issues so that you don't stray significantly from the boss's views on these issues. You are likely to have the opportunity to shape a laissez-faire boss's views and the policy of the organization. Just be sure to do so responsibly, honestly, and carefully.

Country club bosses are so interested in their golf games, the next social event, or their next vacation that they get more and more out of touch. Unlike a laissez-faire boss, who is interested but believes in delegation and empowerment, the country club boss simply has lost interest and may not be willing to help you when you ask for assistance. It may be useful to keep an informal association with the boss at the next level up or, if your boss is the president of the organization, to establish contact with key members of the board of directors, so that you can receive help and support.

Captured-by-the-staff bosses normally have a talented staff that successfully steers the boss around. This can be quite satisfying for the staff, especially if the boss is willing to make decisions and to stick with them. However, this situation can be very frustrating to subordinate leaders in the plants, regional offices, and field activity centers. This is especially bad when the leader makes poor decisions based on faulty or biased staff advice. If you run a facility that is geographically removed from the corporate offices, first attempt to pursue issues through the staff, in hopes of getting staff support for your ideas or initiatives. If this course is not successful, then try to get the boss to meet with you on a regular basis at a place where the staff is not present. This will allow you to lay out your concerns frankly and forthrightly with the boss. Finally, the direct approach with your boss can be helpful in certain circumstances: "We all admire you, but we are having a tough time with your staff." Or perhaps "You have a great staff, but they seem to have lost track of the real world out here."

Big ego bosses only want to hear that what they have done is right. These bosses never want to be challenged about their judgment, wisdom, or decisions. They become defensive when challenged and tend to contradict and threaten anyone who raises criticism. If something good happens, the boss is the cause; if something bad happens, it is always someone else's fault. Avoid direct criticism of this boss. By being very diplomatic, however, a subordinate can plant ideas into the boss's mind that the boss will think are his or her own. When the boss takes full credit for your idea or for the idea of one of your associates, do not challenge the point. However be sure to give yourself some credit and to thank and reward the associate who helped you.

Mother hen bosses give too much specific guidance on even the most routine matters. These bosses treat associates as if they were grammar school children or people of low intelligence. If your

superior is a mother hen boss, ask for a private session and diplo-
matically explain that you are fully capable of doing these routine
tasks with little or no guidance. If this approach is not feasible,
find ways to keep so busy that you do not have time to meet with
the boss for long guidance sessions. A third approach is to suggest
to the boss that he or she handle certain issues so you can concentrate your efforts on other issues. Some mother hen bosses feel
guilty if they are not busy all the time, and this third approach
may help keep them from bothering you with too much advice.

The retired-in-place boss is approaching the end of his or her
career and no longer has much energy for or interest in trying to
do anything new, communicating with associates, or handling
customers' issues. These bosses often can be recognized by their
regular use of the statement "Let's go back to the good old ways
of doing things." Many of these bosses want to enjoy the fruits of
their years of hard work by taking their last year or two off from
any productive involvement in the leadership of the organization.
Try to see this as an opportunity to take initiatives on your own.
If your ideas require the boss to do little or no work, he or she may
accept them. Another approach is to appeal to the boss in terms
of establishing a legacy. Many bosses who are inclined to goof off
will be motivated by a subtle appeal to their egos—a "we would
like to see you retire on a high note" argument. Another useful
approach is to try to get the boss to do a lot of traveling the last year.
This should allow you and your fellow associates to take some
actions while the boss is gone.

Too often, subordinates take a hands-off approach to poor leadership at the top. If the American economic, political, and military
systems are going to thrive in the next century, it is incumbent upon
associates and executives alike to take steps to improve the leadership

of this nation's companies, government agencies, and nonprofit institutions.

Followership and leadership are closely linked. Leaders need good followers; followers need good leaders. Both groups need the positive interaction and chemistry between them if the institution, organization, or company is to thrive. Subordinate associates should remember that no leader wants to fail. No leader wants to be labeled a wimp, a geek, or an autocrat. Those who understand that leadership brings out either the very best or the very worst in an individual, and who are willing to help their leader reach for the best, can be marvelous contributors to excellence and good morale.

You learn a great deal from observing leaders, both good and bad. By seeking and obtaining as many opportunities to exercise leadership as the delegation, empowerment, or apathy of the boss will allow, you can prepare yourself for the great challenges and opportunities that lie ahead. A regular reading program, periodic attendance at executive development seminars, and keeping a file of good quotations, humorous stories, and jokes can help. In addition, actively seek out leadership opportunities in the local community, in church or temple, and in professional associations and clubs. As you work your way up the corporate or institutional ladder, keep in mind that when you become the leader, large numbers of people will be relying on you to be the very best that you can be.

Leading Others

PART II

Leading Others

6

TEACHING, COACHING, MENTORING, AND COUNSELING

Growing Leaders Through New Ideas and Feedback

> It is one of the most beautiful compensations of this life that no man can sincerely try to help another without helping himself.
>
> —*Ralph Waldo Emerson*

Teaching, coaching, mentoring, and counseling are important skills that, when mastered, result in better functioning organizations and more capable and inspired people. While they all target the development of people in learning new skills or knowledge and developing self-awareness, they are different in their approaches.

When we think of teaching, we typically think of experts in the classroom or organization who impart knowledge and share new ideas, concepts, techniques, and information with students. They create an inspired environment for learning—but the burden of learning is on the student.

Coaching has a teaching element for sure, but it is much more focused on training and developing people to achieving certain outcomes or capabilities. Coaches engage in frequent contact with the team members, providing regular feedback.

Mentoring encompasses aspects of teaching and coaching but is generally defined as a formal or informal relationship between a senior mentor (usually outside the protégé's chain of supervision) and a junior protégé.

Counseling, on the other hand, involves one-on-one sessions between a leader and his or her immediate reports. While these sessions provide opportunities for teaching, coaching, and mentoring, the main purpose is to provide a regular review of the employees' progress (or lack of it), the challenges and successes they are facing, and an overview of how the employees (and those who work under them) are furthering the goals and fulfilling the mission of the organization as a whole.

One of the most significant obstacles for any of these approaches is the ability of the leader to ensure that the person he or she is trying to influence does not take constructive criticism personally. A trusted relationship between people will be key to achieving this result.

Teaching

Teaching is a personal responsibility of a good leader, whether you are at the top of the pyramid or have only a single direct report. Major General John Sattler (U.S. Marine Corps) considered teaching to be such an integral part of his leadership philosophy that he had this Daily Self-Assessment message printed on small, wallet-sized cards and disseminated to every Marine in his organization:

> Who did I teach today, and what did I teach them?
> What did I learn today, and who did I learn it from?
> Who did I make smile?

Good leaders tend to be good teachers and to look for opportunities to share the collective wisdom and experience of the organization as well as their own. As a leader, you may teach directly—at staff meetings, briefings for new hires, or one-on-one situations. Your role is not only to impart knowledge but to create environments for people to learn.

Teaching does not always have to take place in a formal setting. Every day you have the opportunity to plant good ideas or present challenges to associates in ways that will encourage them to take ownership of the issues and develop and implement solutions. They may take missteps along the way, but with your subtle guidance, confronting each challenge will be a rewarding and lasting learning experience.

> **The idea of teachable moments is to plant a seed, not to modify behavior, prove a point, or criticize.**
> **—KASS P. DOTTERWEICH**

Learning opportunities should take into account both what employees *want* to know as well as what they *need* to know. A creativity workshop may not appear, at first, to have relevance for a line worker, but whatever contributes to the worker's personal development, to productivity, and to good morale serves a vital purpose.

Every effective organization has formal training programs that address a range of subjects, from learning the processes and procedures, to enhancing communication skills, to creativity. In formal classroom settings or at casual lunch meetings to executive retreats or book clubs, in-house presentations or utilizing outside experts, these ongoing learning sessions should be an integral part of any organization's culture.

Programs for formal teaching, either inside or outside the organization, conducted by in-house personnel or hired consultants, should be made available to employees at all levels. As the leader, you should be aware of what these programs offer, encourage everyone to participate, and explore new programs that would support your vision and mission.

Retreats

A well-run retreat can create one of the more effective learning environments. It can provide opportunities for formal teaching, coaching, mentoring, and counseling all in one. Plus, it provides a venue conducive to enhancing communication, creativity, and teamwork among attendees in a relaxed atmosphere free of office distractions. While retreats are often limited to key personnel, many companies are much more inclusive, depending on how they organize such events. The following pointers are worth keeping in mind no matter what form the retreat may take:

☐ The retreat should become an annual event that goes on everyone's calendar well in advance.

☐ The length of the retreat will vary according to the agenda you determine and accounting for travel distances, etc., but generally two days of uninterrupted time should suffice.

☐ The location should be geographically removed from the normal work area.

☐ The venue should provide a relaxing environment but not offer too many distractions that would tempt attendees to stray.

☐ There need to be clear, well-defined objectives for the event, and they need to be disseminated to the attendees before the event, reviewed with all at the beginning of the event, and then again at the end to provide a graceful conclusion.

☐ Before the retreat, send a short questionnaire to all participants that covers topics such as the high and low points of the year, the new initiatives that the associates would like to take next year, suggested topics of discussion, guest speakers, format, and social events.

☐ All-inclusive leisure activities that promote team involvement should be scheduled in the late afternoon.

☐ Consider having a special guest as the opening speaker from outside the organization, who can help provide some inspiration to the group for why they are gathered and the opportunity they have to make a difference for the future.

☐ Your opening remarks should include:

    ☐ A general statement about the organization's philosophy, goals, priorities, and concerns

    ☐ A review the past year (or time since the previous retreat) that highlights both the ups and the downs

    ☐ A summary of upcoming events or tasks and an explanation of why they are important to the organization

☐ Throughout the retreat you should thank attendees for their outstanding work—and the work of their colleagues back in the office and in the field—and encourage them to seek even higher levels of excellence next year.

☐ Establish guidelines for your sessions so that participants know what to expect and when.

☐ Encourage candor.

☐ Share best practices.

☐ Ask questions that foster discussion such as:

    ☐ What successes have we enjoyed and what have been the secrets to these successes?

    ☐ What is really bothering you about the organization?

    ☐ What opportunities are we missing?

☐ What mistakes have we made or are we making?

☐ How can we make next year more productive?

☐ How could the organization use your time and talents more effectively?

☐ Follow up by asking all participants to share their thoughts about the retreat itself. What did they learn? How could it be more productive next time?

Coaching

Coaching requires a different investment of time and has a different focus. Coaching comes with your job as a leader, especially when you have direct supervisory responsibility over people. You must tailor the agenda and the style of your coaching efforts to achieve the best results for each member of the team in the workplace. Excellence in coaching can usually lead to high-quality people learning the necessary skills to be most effective.

Perry did most of his coaching among fighter pilots in the seven fighter squadrons where he served. His goal was to take young, eager fighter pilots and show them how to be mature flight leaders. This was quite a challenge because younger fighter pilots tend to be free spirits and would prefer spending their time in the air engaging in high-speed dogfights, going supersonic, and flying upside down. Leading a flight of four fighter aircraft into combat is a heavy responsibility. The leader must ensure that everyone in the flight fully understands the tactics, formations, weapons parameters, emergency procedures, and rescue procedures in case of shoot-downs. The leader also must ensure that every pilot is fully ready to take the lead of the flight on a moment's notice. All of this is accomplished by quiet, in-depth coaching.

Like Perry, Jeff's coaching experiences focused on developing the technical and tactical skills of those assigned to his organization. While the Army invests millions of dollars in the formal professional development of soldiers and officers, there is a ton to learn through on-the-job training. Effective coaching and training on the job can make all the difference in the world in building an effective organization. Soldiers are in a perpetual state of learning to be effective at their current pay grade as well as the next pay grade—so the demand is high for caring leaders to invest in them. These same principles apply to most organizations.

Vera Stewart is the president and CEO of Very Vera, a mail-order and local catering service company in Augusta, Georgia, who achieved national recognition after twenty-eight years developing her business. She recently was elected into the Augusta Business Hall of Fame. Among her many exceptional leadership qualities— and her hallmark for success—is her skills as a coach, tireless in her pursuit of constructive, goal-focused development of the character and skills of the members of her team.

Throughout their military careers, both Perry and Jeff were engaged in daily teaching and coaching. They were the teachers and coaches on so many occasions, and were students and members of the team on so many others. The teaching and learning will continue.

Mentoring

> **Help those around you all you can. Every bit of help you give others will come back to you tenfold.**
>
> —E. B. GALLAHER

Mentors are generally those people who voluntarily decide to offer to assist in the professional growth of someone else, typically someone junior or less experienced. It is different from coaching and teaching in that the relationship is created by both parties with the agenda for growth generally driven by the mentee. These relationships are based on periodic engagement—not daily contact. Mentors are often considered lifelong counselors, which indicates that the relationship extends beyond any specific job or task.

Taking care of your people starts their first day on the job. An essential aspect of the hiring process is the welcoming and orientation program that helps the new employee make a smooth and comfortable transition into the organization.

As important as an interviewee's thank-you note following the interview may be, a letter of welcome is most useful and will set the tone for your ongoing working relationship. Many organizations will send an official offer of employment, but that is separate from the letter that you will write.

Aside from your expression of goodwill, this letter will also outline briefly your leadership philosophy and your commitment to high standards of dignity and integrity. As well, it serves a very practical purpose in that it should include the name, address, phone number, and email address of a sponsor, assuming that someone else other than you serves in this role. A sponsor is someone who already works within the same department where the new employee will be assigned.

Most organizations leave the nitty-gritty of orientation to the human resources department since this process involves legal and other technical details, from the compensation package and perks to company guidelines for conduct. However, as the leader, you should welcome new hires and be personally involved in the orientation program. The formality of this process will be determined by a number of factors but should always feature your explicit expression of expectations, your vision for the organization—and the role of the new hire within it. While many of these points will have been discussed during the course of interviews, a new hire will benefit greatly from hearing this message again.

If new employees are graciously welcomed, both in writing and in person, the chances are that they will quickly become fully productive with a good attitude.

It is vital that as the leader you ensure that associates are rewarded properly and that they move on to more senior assignments in a deliberate and thoughtful way. You should identify the very best associates, monitor their careers, encourage the reaching of their potential, and help them attain promotions within the organization.

On the other hand, be very careful not to fall into the trap of cronyism. Being perceived to favor your close friends above others can lead to morale problems. Practicing cronyism can also hurt the very people you are trying to help. If you push a person into a big job before he or she is capable of handling it, or force a friend on a subordinate leader, you often do that individual a great disservice. And if the subordinate leader really does not want the friend, it is likely that your friend's career will suffer in the long run.

The handling of flatterers and bootlickers is an issue related to cronyism. In all large organizations, there are individuals who are very skillful at pleasing the boss by bearing good news and by stroking the boss's ego. They are always looking for ways to make the boss happy, worrying about getting a lot of "face time" with the boss, and serving their own personal ambitions. Unfortunately, there is a direct relationship between cronyism and bootlicking. Leaders must be sensitive to this significant problem area. A good rule of thumb for dealing with bootlickers is to give them some counseling and then send them off to a job that takes them away from the corporate headquarters.

At times unpleasant qualities will emerge in very talented people. One of the worst qualities is arrogance. No matter how talented an individual may be, if he or she becomes arrogant, this person will be unlikely to succeed over the long term as a leader.

Additionally, some individuals who exhibit potential early in their career do not live up to expectations. Leaders who are sponsoring individuals should periodically look at them with a critical eye to be sure that these associates are not dealing with demands that are beyond their capabilities.

A helpful guideline for dealing with your more talented associates is the "one-push rule": give these individuals one strong upward push and then leave them alone. Associates who have truly outstanding talent and potential will keep moving upward with no additional help from you. For those who have reached their ultimate level of potential and competence, further sponsoring them toward higher positions is a mistake. In a comprehensive analysis of why extremely competent young executives get "derailed" on the way to the top, the Center for Creative Leadership in Greensboro, North Carolina, has reported that "over mentoring" often hurts these high achievers.

As a leader, you should pay particular attention to the "late bloomer." Within every organization, there are people of enormous talent who have matured later in life than their contemporaries. Late bloomers need particular attention since personnel managers generally tend to overlook their career potential because their talent was either not evident or not recognized at an earlier time in their career.

Many leaders make the mistake of confining their mentoring to those on the executive track. Mentoring also consists of identifying the best of the people at the lowest level and giving them compliments and a boost. You must ensure that the organization is not neglecting or abusing the associates at lower levels—the people with the least power. You should consider establishing a formal mentoring program so that certain associates don't get left without a mentor. Racial and gender minorities especially will appreciate the care and support received from their mentors.

George Marshall probably provides the best model in the area of constructive mentoring. He had identified people of great talent and potential during the first thirty-five years of his Army career. Marshall had a carefully compiled list of outstanding people in the Army and the Army Air Corps. When President Franklin Delano Roosevelt selected him to be the chief of staff of the Army in 1939, Marshall used this list when selecting individuals for key staff and command positions in the immediate prewar period. When war broke out, he used this list extensively to pick the top wartime leaders. To a very large extent, the U.S. military did extremely well in World War II because of General Marshall's prudent sponsorship of people of character who had great leadership potential.

More recent examples of outstanding mentors include Jack Welch of General Electric and Dr. Robert Langer of MIT. During the twenty years that Welch was CEO of General Electric, he identified and groomed a number of individuals who moved on to run some of the largest and most successful corporations in America. Dr. Langer provides a marvelous example of outstanding mentorship. Langer, who heads the Langer Institute at MIT, has an amazing record of accomplishment, leadership, and vision. Not only does he have more than eight hundred patents in his name but he has also mentored many students and associates who now are in top leadership positions in the high-tech world.

Finally, there is a close relationship between successful mentoring and the promotion of associates. Leaders of large organizations should provide guidance to subordinate leaders and personnel managers concerning the criteria for promotion. The promotion system must be not only fair, but also perceived to be so. Select members of promotion panels very carefully. Then give specific written guidance to each panel. Also, prior to the time when it convenes, meet privately with the head of the promotion board. After the board completes its work, the head should report back to the leader and state specifically where the board was unable to carry out fully its guidance.

Counseling

Encourage your staff to be candid with you. Ask their advice and listen to it. Top bananas have no monopoly on ideas.
—DAVID OGILVY

Most mid- to large-size organizations have formal annual performance evaluation systems in place. While "performance counseling" may address many of the same issues as a review or evaluation, its purpose is much more wide-ranging, and perhaps more valuable to both the employee and the organization, since it doesn't carry the stigma of an "evaluation" or "review."

About once every six months or so, depending on the circumstances, you will want to set up one-on-one sessions with those associates who work directly for you. These sessions provide an opportunity for you to share your overview of the company as a whole and how your associate (and his or her group) are fitting in and fulfilling their goals and mission. They are also the occasion for your direct reports to addresses issues, both positive and negative, about the associate's own performance and that of the division. Most important, the purpose of these sessions is to exchange ideas and insights in a quiet and focused way.

For you as the leader, it is the time to offer praise and encouragement along with advice. For associates, these sessions should provide the chance get the full attention of the boss on important personal and organizational issues.

Although many leaders may talk about how they counsel their people, in actuality effective counseling sessions seldom take place.

A quick meeting in the hall, a brief comment or two at a staff meeting, or a passing remark here and there do not constitute good counseling. Sometimes, however, if an employee makes a serious mistake or a critical situation arises that clearly requires immediate corrective action, avoid public admonishment and set up a private meeting as quickly as possible.

Effective long-term counseling can only happen when both parties are prepared to focus on important issues in an atmosphere of trust and cooperation. A truly effective counseling session balances the discussions of strengths and weakness, of ideas and aspirations. While it should take place in a relaxed and friendly atmosphere, you have to set personalities and personal agendas aside and focus on the key issues that affect your employee, your organization, and you.

A few pointers to keep in mind that will make the process work best for everyone include:

- Schedule counseling sessions as regularly as possible. Once every six months is probably ideal.

- Make the appointment for a counseling session far enough in advance so that you and your associate have time to prepare.

- Set aside at least one hour for a session. While some may be shorter, you do not want to give short shrift to important issues that arise during the meeting.

- Establish an agenda based on the series of questions that appear in this chapter. But be flexible and tailor your discussions to the individual's needs.

- Start and end each session on a positive note. Even if an individual has been struggling or underperforming, you need to give the individual hope that things can improve. After all, that is the point of the counseling.

The following list of questions can act as a good guideline for a discussion. The annotation included for some of the questions are to help you in guiding the interview. You may, in fact, which to adapt this list according to your needs and share it with your associate in advance of your one-on-one. In doing so, you will ensure that both of you come to the session prepared to focus on the vital issues that affect both the individual's performance and the health of the organization. Your associate will better understand your expectations for this meeting, and being able to prepare, he or she will be more at ease.

Which aspects of this organization do you like the most?

It is useful to start the session on a positive note. This question can be an icebreaker since the associate may be a bit uncomfortable during the first few minutes in a private meeting with the boss.

What issues concern you most?

This question allows the associate to voice those areas of real heartburn. It might be that the associate does not like the job, the work hours, the level of authority, the living conditions, the pay, or the amount of recognition received. It is a good opportunity to smoke out those things that really bother your associates. How can you improve this organization? As a leader, you are in charge not only of gathering ideas, but also of finding out where the "idea people" are. In every organization, there are some people who are especially useful and innovative. This question often helps identify a person who is deeply committed to improving the organization and who has the talents to make things happen.

What personal goals have you set for yourself?

You want to encourage associates to express their aspirations. Some will prefer to stay at their current levels (for the present or near future); others will want to move to another division or location; still others will want to move upward. You will be able to consider your employees' short- and long-range plans within the context of the whole organization and utilize this information in your overall personnel strategy.

Equally important, you can help an associate who does not have specific goals to develop them.

Where and to what job would you like to go next? Why? When?

This line of questioning gives you an opportunity to have individuals evaluate their own potential for moving up to higher levels of responsibility. You will find out whether their expectations are realistic. If they do have inflated expectations and you are aware of weak or mediocre professional records, you can give them a candid appraisal. It is important that you be frank as well as factual so that individuals with poor performance records are prepared if they fail to be promoted at some later date. Any assessment on your part of the person's prospects should also be tempered with advice on how the person can improve his or her chances of advancement.

What do you consider to be your most significant weaknesses?

If individuals are not forthcoming about where they think they're falling short, you may have a problem right there. As often happens, the individual may outline personal weaknesses fairly well, but might miss one or two areas that you consider important. This gives you the opportunity to discuss a range of abilities, from the individual's written or verbal and presentation skills to his or her comfort level dealing with subordinates or cooperating with peers. Although these are delicate issues, following this line of questioning often opens the door to excellent counseling opportunities.

What self-improvement programs do you have under way?
There are so many opportunities open to employees, from company-sponsored workshops and learning session, to advanced degree programs, to a wide range of self-improvement classes. Many of these opportunities are subsidized wholly or in part by an organization. You have to question why an individual who has articulated his or her most significant weakness is not taking some action to overcome them.

What three things that you are required to do cause you to waste your time the most?

What goals have you established for the division for which you are responsible?
Do the individual's goals conform to the ones that have been established for the whole organization? Perhaps the individual has established goals that are more thoughtful or innovative than your own.

How has your division performed over the past six months? What were the high and low points of the period?
This is a useful way to ascertain the objectivity of subordinate leaders when it comes to their own areas. You can also get an idea of how willing they are to take responsibility for setbacks, as well as to whom or what they attribute any impressive successes.

Have any of my decisions or policies or my leadership style failed to support your performance or that of your division?
Encouraging criticism is a brave act. But giving your associates the opportunity to voice their opinions openly in an atmosphere of confidence and trust will lead to many positive outcomes. If an associate is prepared for you to ask this question, the associate will certainly have to be ready to back up his or her opinions with the facts as the

associate sees them. As with any questions of such a delicate nature, you don't want to become defensive, but rather you want to bring your best listening skills into play.

Who are the most innovative, helpful, and cooperative people in this organization?

Asking your associate to identify his or her best coworkers will help you identify the most valuable employees who may not be your direct reports. It is not unusual that someone who is particularly quiet, for example, might be identified as a key contributor.

A corollary to this question may be the more delicate one: Are there individuals who you feel are not pulling their weight, are uncooperative, causing problems, or not performing up to their potential?

What are your ideas for improving this organization?

This question provides an opening for a much bigger discussion about the organization as a whole and to hear from associates what things they feel are inhibiting the accomplishment of the organization's mission. This question may introduce a discussion of policies, procedures, systems, tactics, and subordinate organizations, and, on a corporate scale, considerations for divestitures and acquisitions.

In your life, what recognition that you received did you value the most?

The answer to this question will be helpful when it is time to salute or reward this individual. Some will say a gentle pat on the back. Others will say a public event where they received a present or an award. Others will say a nice bonus check. Others will say an unexpected promotion. Others will say a personal, handwritten note. This is the best way to find out what each individual working for you really appreciates in the way of praise.

Is there anything that this organization can do for you, for your family, or for community affairs in which you are interested?
While questions of a personal nature always need to be handled with great delicacy, it is important to show that your organization is prepared to support its employees in any number of areas, from health and wellness programs to charitable or cultural endeavors.

7

BUILDING YOUR LEADERSHIP MODEL

A Framework for You and Your Associates

■ ■ ■

Life is a challenge, meet it.
Life is a duty, complete it.
Life is a promise, fulfill it.
Life is an adventure, dare it.

—*Mother Teresa*

If you want your life to be a magnificent story, then begin by realizing that you are the author and every day you have the opportunity to write a new page.

—*Mark Houlahan*

The U.S. Army established a model framework for leader development that is universally applicable and consists of three components: formal education and training, on-the-job experience, and self-development. This chapter focuses on how to take what you have learned from all three components and tie it together in a leadership model that fits you, your personality, and your goals.

In his classic book *How to Win Friends and Influence People*, Dale Carnegie made it clear that to become a better leader, you must "possess a deep driving desire to learn, a vigorous determination to increase your ability to deal with people." And Ken Blanchard and Mark Miller echo this idea in their book *Great Leaders Grow*: "The path to increased influence, impact, and leadership effectiveness is paved with personal growth."

While some people are blessed with certain genetic or inherent advantages, great leaders develop over time with ceaseless learning and the application of what they learn when dealing with everyone and everything in an organization.

Learning is an active process. Most of our learning comes through day-to-day experiences, taking actions and making decisions without really examining the rationale for what we did and why we did it. If you want to become a better, more effective leader, it is worthwhile to consider developing a more disciplined, deliberate approach to learning. One of the most effective ways to learn involves a five-step process:

1. Create your model for leading.

2. Act on that model.

3. Assess the results.

4. Modify your model based on these assessments.

5. Modify your behavior accordingly.

There are a host of options for leadership models, from many popular programs. One of our favorite models comes from *The Secret: What Great Leaders Know and Do* by Ken Blanchard and Mark Miller. In this book the authors present a model based with the acronym SERVE:

See the future.

Engage and develop others.

Reinvent continuously.

Value results and relationships.

Embrace the values.

It is important, however, to develop a model that fits your personality *and* meets the needs of the organization. When Jeff was asked many years ago how he would characterize his leadership philosophy, he was not sure how to answer. He had never given it much thought. But the question prompted him to develop what he would soon call his model. As he went through the ranks in the Army, he collected feedback, reassessed his positions, and over time, his effectiveness as a leader improved.

Jeff's model for leading took on different forms over the years. At times it was a list of top ten important tasks. At other times, it included a personal mission statement or the expression of a command philosophy. Each refinement and addition to his model was based on his years of personal experience and input that he got from coaches and mentors, leadership development programs, and his own reading of books and articles on leadership. His current model of leadership features nine components:

1. Be a leader of character.

2. Create an effective leadership environment.

3. Establish a vision.

4. Develop a plan.

5. Establish and stay focused on priorities.

6. Seek assistance from advisors and counselors.

7. Be a perpetual optimist.

8. Maintain a sense of humor.

9. Embrace those in need.

Perry's model was largely based on his experience as a fighter pilot. Because fighter aircraft fly in small formations of two or four airplanes, there are many leaders within every fighter squadron. Young pilots are given the responsibility to plan missions, brief their wingmen, and carry out the missions safely and efficiently. Even in a combat environment, the flight leaders are often young Air Force captains who have not yet reached the age of thirty. The entire fighter pilot culture is based on the assumption that in a crisis or combat situation, the youngest and most inexperienced wingman might, in a split second, have to assume the leadership of the entire flight. Hence every new fighter pilot is trained as a leader from the very first day he or she checks into a fighter squadron. Quite early in his military career, Perry learned that through excellent training, close mentorship, and mutual respect, young people could perform superbly even under the most stressful conditions. His leadership model evolved into one of empowerment and trust that was supported by eight pillars:

1. Hire the very best people.

2. Guide them so that they understand and fully support the mission.

3. Train them rigorously.

4. Grant them your trust by giving them lots of responsibility and authority.

5. Give them credit for the successes of the organization.

6. Take personal responsibility for the setbacks.

7. Have fun and never postpone joy.

8. Constantly thank people for their good work.

You can develop your own personal leadership model. Make it a list that comprises clearly defined and measurable goals that will work for you and your organization. Adopt a model from the contents of this book or another favorite leadership program. Adapt the philosophy of a leader you respect. Do not be too concerned about perfecting it—just do it. Capture it; document it; put it to work. Share it with other trusted members of your team, coaches, advisors, mentors, or friends. By reflecting on your own behavior and keeping track of your progress in a journal or through periodic debriefings with yourself, you will learn more about your own strengths—and weaknesses—and how you deal with people under a variety of conditions. Use this reflection and other assessments of your behavior to determine if and how you should adjust your model. This process will help you become a better leader. Sharing your lessons with others will help them become better leaders, too.

FOR FURTHER READING

How to Win Friends and Influence People by Dale Carnegie
The Secret: What Great Leaders Know and Do by Ken Blanchard and Mark Miller
Great Leaders Grow: Becoming a Leader for Life by Ken Blanchard and Mark Miller
Smart Thinking: Three Essential Keys to Solve Problems, Innovate, and Get Things Done by Art Markman, PhD

8

HIRING

Putting the Right People in the Right Jobs

in the Right Way

■ ■ ■

Recipe for success: First, make a reputation for creative genius. Second, surround yourself with partners who are better than you are. Third, leave them to get on with it.

—*David Ogilvy*

First get the right people on the bus (and the wrong people off the bus) and then figure out where to drive it.

—*Jim Collins*

As a leader, one of your most important responsibilities is the recruitment and selection of the best possible candidates who will serve you and your organization with distinction.

The Search

In most large organizations, the search will be directed by the human resources professionals, in-house or hired. But it is your responsibility to ensure that these individuals fully understand the criteria for the position. The better you communicate your needs and wishes to those on the front lines of searching and screening candidates, the more efficient the process will be.

In certain circumstances, especially for high-level or key positions, you may establish a search committee comprising associates from different parts of the company who will be affected by this new hire. The members of this committee may have expertise and perspective that you don't have and will raise the most relevant issues and ask the most revealing questions. Along with your human resources department, you can use this committee to screen out and reduce the list to a manageable number, but, ultimately, you will be making the final decision.

You may also participate in the search personally, using your network of contacts. Your peers in other organizations may have some suitable candidates or they might provide valuable insights on the candidates you are considering. Social media, such as LinkedIn, Facebook, and Twitter can be worthwhile tools for screening candidates. Candidates tend to be more candid on social media than on their résumés. The information on these forums may provide a broader perspective on their activities, interests, and aspirations. But when it comes to social media, you have to be cautious when engaging with prospective hires, given the public nature of these sites. Always seek advice from your professional recruiters to avoid any legal situations or awkwardness in dealing with applicants.

While the basic requirements of education and experience will be detailed in any posted job description, it is the intangibles that will separate the merely qualified candidates from your final choice. Generally only the personal interview will allow you to obtain the broadest picture of the candidate.

The Interview

There is no question that when it comes to the final stage of selection—the interview—you will have to participate when hiring a direct report. You may have benefited from the input of your HR people or your search committee, but you need to be prepared for that one-on-one interview that will be critical to your decision.

It is not uncommon for the interview to include some of your colleagues. You may want to ask one or two of your most trusted associates to sit in on the interview. Such partners in the process can add an important dimension to the interview since they may have a valuable depth of experience with the process and may provide different perspectives. Your associates may, in fact, act as the final screening before the candidate comes to you.

However you orchestrate the interview, you will have ensured that candidates have been fully vetted before they step into your office. You will want to ensure that each candidate fulfills all the basic criteria for the position. Just as importantly, can the candidate generate that indefinable quality of "chemistry" that will help determine how well an individual will fit into the environment of your organization? But one caution about chemistry is in order. In seeking associates with the right chemistry, there is always the danger that prejudices and biases of which you may not even be aware will sway your decision. Be careful not to use "bad chemistry" as an excuse for rejecting a well-qualified candidate who may come from a different cultural, social, or educational background from you. This is a slippery slope and one in which your human resources professionals and associates should provide appropriate sounding boards.

While each interview will be unique to the people and circumstances, every interview should be conducted systematically. A checklist of questions to ask appears at the end of this chapter, but some of the most important questions are explored below:

Why Do You Want This Job?

This should be the first question you ask of prospective employees. If they express anything but enthusiasm, indicate any serious reservations, or have motivations that you do not find useful or particularly attractive, the interview can be wrapped up quickly and the individual eliminated from consideration. If you are satisfied and impressed by the response, continue the interview.

Why Should I Hire You?

This question should elicit the candidates' own perceptions about their strengths and what they can contribute to the company. So you may wish to follow this question with one that is directed to a candidate's perceived weaknesses. Rarely will interviewees discuss their weaknesses, unless they are prompted to do so. But these questions are very useful in determining how introspective the individual is. If the candidate articulates a great many strengths and admits to no weaknesses (or better stated as "areas of performance that need attention"), you may have identified an individual who will not serve you well. Someone who not only outlines strengths but also is aware of and working on weaknesses probably deserves serious consideration. Neither a candidate who is arrogantly self-assured nor one who lacks fundamental self-confidence is likely to be a major contributor to your organization.

How Would Your Present Associates Describe Your Leadership Style?

The response to this question can reveal the attitude that the individual has toward subordinates as well as their own analysis of his or her leadership style. In combination with what you find out from other sources, you can assess how well this candidate grasps the interpersonal realities of his or her present situation.

What Values Do You Esteem and Why?

An interviewee's answer to this question should give you a feeling for how deeply he or she has thought about the subject. Answers involving high integrity, character, concern for others, altruism, and service above self will tell you one thing. Answers that discuss job fulfillment or opportunities for promotion will tell you something else. Your follow-up questions may give you a helpful understanding of what drives the interviewee.

What Is the Toughest Problem You Have Ever Faced? How Did You Handle It?

These questions can be a useful way to determine to what extent individuals have been tested and what they have learned from a difficult experience. You may gain some insights about how candidates deal with failure and whether they can function under pressure.

Who in Your Present Organization Do You Respect the Most and Why?

This question provides insights into what candidates think are the important aspects of leadership. If they admire a strong leader and know why, it is likely that they know what leadership qualities they would like to emulate.

What Is It That Concerns You in Your Present Organization?

In responding to this question, candidates may reveal aspects about their interaction within the organization that will reinforce your desire to hire the person, or, conversely, give you indications that you would not be comfortable with this individual. (This is also a key question that you may ask of a candidate from within your organization who is seeking a new placement.)

What Are the Standards of Integrity in Your Present Organization?

How candidates judge their present employer will reflect on their own standards of personal integrity. In fact, it will reveal whether they think or care much about integrity. This can lead to a useful discussion on the issues of institutional and personal ethics and the role that these qualities play within an organization.

If You Were in Charge of This Organization, What Steps Would You Take to Improve Its Performance?

Candidates who have reached the interview stage in the hiring process should already have done their homework and should have a basic understanding of the operation and the issues that your organization faces. A question like this will reveal how seriously they have prepared for the interview. The answer should also reveal if they have original ideas and insights, as well as a willingness to speak up about aspects of the organization that they find inadequate. This question also calls for a high level of diplomacy since you are asking candidates to be as forthright as they can in offering suggestions for change, especially given the limited knowledge they may have about your organization. It will also reveal where a candidate sits on the spectrum of confidence and arrogance.

What Are Your Long-Term Personal Goals?

Long-term goals should not be stated in terms of how long a person will stay in your organization but rather in terms of how they see fulfilling their own career ambitions, whether it is within the organization or not. Only you can determine if the candidate appears overly ambitious, unwilling to "pay his or her dues," or will always be on the lookout for the next opportunity to advance. While a candidate's past performance may not always be an accurate predictor of what he or she will do in the future, factors such as how long the candidate has stayed at previous jobs, how he or she progressed within another organization, or his or her reasons for leaving often speak louder than whatever goals the candidate may declare.

What Are the Best Books and Professional Journals That You Have Read? What Insights Did You Gain from These Readings?

Knowing what people read for their professional growth—and what they've learned—will tell you how intellectually curious they are and how open they are to the ideas, suggestions, and insights that good books and periodicals can provide. And, of course, you will want to be assured that they are keeping up with their discipline or profession. Along with reading, other endeavors of continual learning, such as courses and workshops, are critical to one's personal and professional development. Those who don't make use of these are unlikely to grow and contribute beyond the level of their present competence.

Is There Anything That Would Be Helpful for Me to Know Now That Might Be an Embarrassment If It Surfaces Later?

Such a question needs to be asked particularly if the position for which this person is applying is high-profile or politically sensitive. People applying for these kinds of jobs may be subject to background checks in any event, but it is very important to determine how candid the individual is willing to be. You may want to hire the person regardless of the response, but it's vital to have all of the cards on the table.

If You Are Not Selected for This Position, Who Would You Recommend?

Such a question will reveal how the person judges the job and the qualities that are needed for it, and how closely the applicant is in contact with other individuals with similar qualifications. It also will bring out how willing the individual is to acknowledge that there may be others who are as qualified—or better qualified—for the job.

What Questions That I Have Not Asked Would You Like Me to Ask?

Some candidates will have some vital information that they would like to share if only they were asked. For instance, they may have a family issue, a health issue, or an issue relating to when they might be able to join your organization if they were hired.

Hiring Checklist

When you are hiring someone for a key position, a well-constructed personal interview will allow you to get a sense of the candidate that few résumés can provide. It is rare that anything but a face-to-face interview will suffice, although in exceptional circumstances a telephone interview may be an acceptable substitute.

The following questions provide a good reminder list for conducting the interview, keeping it on track, and yielding responses that will reveal a lot about the interviewee.

Many of these questions have been explored in greater detail above, but to one degree or another they are all important. The order in which you ask these questions will be dictated by the individual circumstances of each interview, but using these questions as a guideline will help you get the most out of the time that you have with each potential candidate:

Why do you want this job?

Why should I hire you?

What talents, qualities, and strengths can you bring to this organization and to this job in particular?

What do you see as your greatest weaknesses?

What experience do you have with the following areas?
- Operations
- Planning
- Finance/marketing
- Research and development
- Training
- Computer systems
- Human resource management

How many people have you led or supervised in your career?

How would you describe your leadership/management style?

If I asked one of your associates to describe you and your leadership style, what would be the response?

Have you had any setbacks in your life? If so, what were the most significant lessons learned from the setbacks?

What organizational setbacks have you observed firsthand?

What is it that concerns you in your present organization?

What is the toughest problem that you have faced in your professional career? How did you handle it?

What are your long-term personal goals?

Is there anything that would be helpful for me to know now that might be an embarrassment if it surfaces later?

What are the best books that you have read in the last few years? What insights did they provide you?

What are the standards of integrity in your present organization?

In your present organization, whom do you admire the most and why?

Are you considering any other positions?

If I select you for this job, will you take it as your first choice over the other positions that you are considering?

If you are not selected, whom would you recommend for this job?

What questions have I failed to ask you?

What questions do you have for me?

9

INSPIRING YOUR PEOPLE

Establishing and Maintaining Joy

■ ■ ■

Those who truly lead are able to create a following of people who act not because they were swayed but because they were inspired. For those who are inspired, the motivation to act is deeply personal.

—*Simon Sinek*

Motivating and inspiring your people—how do you do it? What is the secret? What do people need that you, as their leader, must provide for them to be inspired? How do you create that "something special" in your organization that enables this inspiration to take place? Good questions all. The ability to inspire is clearly one of those rare traits that separate great leaders from good ones.

What People Need

Experts in the fields of psychiatry, psychology, neuroscience, and other human behavior analysts have documented the fundamental "needs" of people. The American philosopher Dr. John Dewey, best known for his views on educational reform, claimed that the "deepest urge in human nature is the desire to be important." And Dr. Viktor Frankl, Austrian neurologist and psychiatrist and Holocaust survivor, wrote: "Striving to find a meaning in one's life—that is the primary, most powerful motivating and driving force in humans."

Lou Holtz, the College Hall of Fame football coach and world-class motivational speaker, expressed human need this way: "Everyone needs something to do, someone to love, something to hope for, someone to believe in." The message common to these assessments is that effective leaders understand and do all they can to meet these needs.

Most people must work to earn a paycheck to provide for their families, pay leases or mortgages, plan for college for their children, and take care of aging parents. In many environments, financial incentives have a significant impact on people's willingness to reach higher and go the extra mile to meet certain goals. But long-term, sustained inspiration will not be met by financial incentives alone.

People need to know you care about them. There is a great saying, attributed to John C. Maxwell: "People do not care how much you know until they know how much you care." If the leader does not care about the employee, you can be sure that the employee will not care about the leader, and subsequently will be uninspired to work harder.

People need to know where they fit in the overall mission of the organization. They need to understand and be committed to the vision, the mission, and the values of the organization. All members of the team must understand their individual roles and how they fit into the overall team's role.

People need to be able to trust their fellow employees and the leadership of the organization. If there is no trust, the members of that team will simply not want to perform. People need to know they are being treated fairly and equitably—both elements are keys to achieving trust. Have you ever been in a position where you did not trust your partners or leaders? How did it make you feel? What was that climate like? There may be periods of time in which members of the organization tolerate unacceptable environments, such as lack of trust, if they believe that the condition will pass. But it is a risky proposition to think that if such an environment is sustained, the workforce will still be motivated to perform at a high standard.

Members of your workforce range in skill levels from rookies to seasoned veterans. Each member of your team has strengths that need to be determined and then cultivated. And for many of your people there will be limits on their capability (and desire) to serve at various leadership levels of the organization. These differences in the individuals on your team make it paramount that you really know them. You need to tailor your approaches accordingly to increase the potential to achieve the best results from them.

All will need some element of coaching—a task that is part of your job as a leader. As a coach, you drive the agenda to help achieve better performance in the workplace. To serve your team best is to understand who merits the investment of time and energy, determine how they can best serve the organization, and put into place the programs that will enable the organization to capitalize on that service. Faculty members at a university who desire to become department heads need to know there is a program in place that can help them be successful in that new role. Same for members of an assembly line who desire to be shift supervisors and for sales representatives who desire to become sales managers. Leader development programs are vitally important for organizations, to help further these transitions and growth opportunities for their people. For those people who either cannot or have no desire to produce, other decisions need to be made regarding their future with the organization.

Today's workplace holds multiple generations, from Baby Boomers to Gen Xers, to Millennials, to Generation "Always On" (referring to the youth of today, influenced by access to the world via the Internet, Twitter, Facebook, etc.). While each of these groups may be inspired by different motives, all these folks, like all other people, still seek to be a well-integrated part of an organization and to know that their leaders genuinely care about them.

How to Serve the Needs of Your People

Your can best serve the needs of the majority of the members of your workforce by finding a way to touch their hearts. Understanding their needs—above and beyond the salary and benefits you pay—is your number one task. Once you determine their true needs, you can proceed with addressing them. But harsh or thoughtless treatment of your people doesn't work well in today's world—if it ever did!

Listening

Leaders must learn to be fully engaged listeners: an apt phrase is "squinting with the ears." They should look directly and intensely into the eyes of the person who is speaking. Leaders must have inquisitive minds—a thirst for knowledge. They need to get out and interact with the workforce and listen when messages are being transmitted their way. Jeff will always remember when, as a young lieutenant, he was asked by his company commander, Captain Thom Tuckey, for his recommendation on what punishment should be imposed on a soldier for his misconduct. As it turned out, the captain listened to Jeff's recommendation, based his decision on that recommendation, and Jeff instantly became more inspired, knowing that he had a credible voice in the organization. Jeff applied that lesson of listening and trusting throughout his military and post-military career. That was just one of many lessons he learned from Captain Tuckey.

Listening is the most important skill of effective leaders. Introverts have a great edge, since they tend to listen quietly and usually aren't "interruptaholics." Too many extroverts are thinking about what they will say next rather than hearing what is being said now. This is called "fake listening." Whereas introverts are natural listeners, extroverts need help in gaining and maintaining this essential skill. All extroverts should read and heed *Just Listen: Discover the Secret of Getting Through to Absolutely Anyone* by Mark Goulston.

If a leader is a good listener, he or she can accept ideas, criticism, and other feedback that can improve the organization and create an atmosphere of excellence and caring. In the words of an unknown sage, "I never learned anything while I was talking."

As leaders move up in the ranks, they become more and more ignorant of the day-to-day activities below them because the subordinate leaders naturally want to fix everything possible before it reaches the boss. So the burden falls on senior leaders to do what is necessary to stay in touch with their people. Often a great technique is simply walking around and personally engaging people throughout the organization—sometimes referred to as Leading by Walking Around (LBWA). When leaders personally engage their workforce in the team's own environment, it is a clear indication that the leadership cares, as long as it is a sincere visit and follow-up actions are taken when necessary. When leaders demonstrate a sincere desire to learn more about their associates, their families, their work environment, and the issues that are especially important to their people, the dividends for both the boss and the workforce can be huge. If an issue is raised by an employee, and later taken care of by the leader through action, a powerful message is sent throughout the organization.

Engagement

This is a common technique used by John Stewart, the plant manager at the Bridgestone Tire Manufacturing Plant in Aiken, South Carolina. John regularly engages his people on the plant floor, for about an hour each morning and most afternoons. It is not simply a walk—it is a walk with a purpose—and a clear demonstration to the Bridgestone team that he cares. This plant has earned a host of awards and accolades for production and safety since opening in 1997, including being named one of *Industry Week*'s Top 10 Manufacturers in the United States (only five years after the plant opened). During his tour of the facility, Jeff felt camaraderie throughout the enormous plant.

By listening intently to the employees, Jeff found out what caused them to join and, more importantly, why they stayed on "Workforce Bridgestone." John Stewart had grown up in the facility, starting at its opening, and was promoted to plant manager in 2009. As Jeff toured the facility with him, Jeff could sense a powerful, positive leadership. The responses Jeff got when he asked what the employees liked best about Bridgestone would make any leader proud—with one in particular standing out: "I get a good salary to provide for my family, the leadership ensures I have a safe place to work, and I know they care about me—that I have a voice that will be heard."

Accountability

Tough love is a term often used for enforcing standards and holding people accountable for their obligations as members of a team. The members of the team want to know that they are all being held to the same standard and there are clear consequences when standards are not met. Fairness—in rewards and punishments—is key to ensuring efficient organizations. While the reinforcement of positive behaviors is always the preferred way to inspire, there are times when taking appropriate immediate disciplinary action is necessary, especially when safety or other critical aspects of an organization's mission are at risk. Everyone needs to understand that excellence matters—that it takes hard work and commitment to be the very best one can be and that these qualities are the only way the organization will be successful. The strength of an organization will grow, and respect for the leadership will grow, when timely action is taken to fix problems.

Empathy

Weddings are optional, funerals are mandatory.
—RUDOLPH W. GIULIANI IN *LEADERSHIP*

In the weeks and months after the Twin Towers were destroyed on September 11, 2001, Mayor Giuliani attended many, many funerals. This task certainly never appeared in the job description for a mayor of America's largest city, but it was as integral a part of his position as making sure public transportation was running, keeping the crime rate down, or balancing the budget. Caring leaders understand the power and grace of caring. In fact, Giuliani's empathy became a part of his legacy of leadership in a way that no other action he took could.

In the latest version of the U.S. Army's Manual on Leadership (FM 6-22, Army Leadership, October 2006), empathy is given its due importance as an essential character attribute of a leader. It is important for leaders to recognize the needs of soldiers and families during challenging times of trauma or suffering, ultimately helping the family cope or to obtain the help they need. This skill targets the "care factor" and its inclusion in the manual demonstrates its importance for the Army. How to embrace those in need depends on the situation—but the best leaders find a way.

Acknowledging your employees' personal challenges outside the workplace will demonstrate how much you truly care for them.

Gratitude

The happiness of life is made up of minute fractions . . . a smile, a kind look, or a heartfelt compliment.
—SAMUEL TAYLOR COLERIDGE

In most organizations, more than 90 percent of the people are working diligently to accomplish the mission, to serve the institution, and to make the organization look good, or to make you look good. People generally want to associate with, and participate in, success. It is important to remind yourself often that your people are working hard and doing a fine job.

Expressing simple, heartfelt, and specific praise can motivate people to perform at higher levels of excellence and cooperation. This is especially true when those compliments are well timed and well phrased. Conversely, your failure to acknowledge work well done can be devastating to an organization. Too many leaders take the attitude that their people are "only doing their job" and "that's what they get paid for." The hidden price is low morale and a reduced level of performance.

Catch people doing things right—and acknowledge it privately and publicly. The rewards and returns of immediate recognition are immeasurable and pervasive. While your organization may have formal ways in which to celebrate accomplishments—awards, prizes, medals, or bonuses—it is the everyday gesture—a personal handwritten note, verbal praise in a meeting, notification in the company newsletter—that will have an enduring effect. Immediately reward those individuals and groups that do something extraordinary or something ordinary in an extraordinary way or with great results. Don't postpone joy.

Foster an environment of gratitude. Pass your compliments down the line through your associates. Praise one group's accomplishments to others, not as a stick to make an underperforming group feel bad, but as an incentive and model from which all can learn. Everyone wants to be acknowledged publicly. Encourage those groups and individuals who aren't to seek out ways to make it onto the list, to discover and use the best practices that are available to them.

Finally, a leader also must know how to accept compliments. Sharing every compliment with your associates should be your first instinct. After all, in almost every case, the success was also theirs— their ideas, their efficiency, their hard work, and their creativity.

Accepting Failure

Accepting that even the best people will make mistakes is a very important element in developing the trust and confidence of your people. Jeff's command philosophy while in charge of Army organizations was "Honest mistakes in the pursuit of excellence are okay." This statement confirmed his willingness to underwrite mistakes. He understood that risks need to be taken and that lessons learned by mistakes can be powerful opportunities for growth. When people know that you are willing to underwrite honest mistakes they will be more willing to take initiatives to improve the organization.

Optimism

> **Spare me the grim litany of the "realist"; give me the unrealistic aspirations of the optimist any day.**
> —COLIN POWELL

Be a perpetual optimist—it is contagious. If a leader is positive and engaged, that attitude will often spread throughout the organization. A positive environment can make bad things not so bad, and make good things better. How do you feel when you walk through the door of your organization? A leader's positive thinking helps inspire others. This positive climate brings inner peace to people, helps improve relationships, and creates an opportunity for better health and enjoyment in life. Your people will be more responsive, more willing to collaborate, and ultimately more inspired to reach higher performances if they work in this type of work setting.

Positive Attitude

You are not only the chief executive but also the head cheerleader. If you love your job, be sure to share that fact with your associates. If you have genuine affection for those who work for you, be sure to tell them. As the leader, knowing how to laugh, especially at yourself, can be a great enabler of personal rapport. Even a smile alone can often diffuse a very intense situation and can help turn a mistake into a learning opportunity. Appropriate humor in the workplace promotes a positive attitude throughout the organization. (The emphasis here is on "appropriate" humor—that doesn't belittle or demean others, inside or outside your organization.)

Expressing a positive attitude does not mean you become the company Pollyanna. You do have to recognize the challenges that your organization faces, but it is your job not only to discover or enable solutions but to ensure that your people are inspired even in difficult circumstances.

If you have associates who are cynical and pessimistic, give them lots of one-on-one time to vent and criticize. But take this opportunity to share with them your concern that their negative attitude may be damaging the morale and esprit of the organization.

Celebrate

Celebrate the victories—whenever and wherever possible. So often we are so caught up in the day-to-day operations or deadlines that we forget to take time to acknowledge the great work done by the people who earned the victories. Make time for these events. Be innovative with how you thank people and how you recognize them. Allocate time on the calendar to ensure the celebratory event is not overlooked or forgotten. If there is no funding in the budget to support the event, reach into your own pocket to pay for the celebration. The word will spread and your generosity will be deeply appreciated.

Thank-You Checklist

There are many reasons that your associates deserve your thanks. This checklist is a reminder of the ways in which you can express your gratitude every day. Sometimes we simply forget to do them.

Thank you for your:

☐ Contribution to the mission.

☐ Honesty and integrity.

☐ Professionalism, commitment to excellence, and for setting and maintaining high standards.

☐ Selfless service and dedication.

☐ Leadership.

☐ Help in meeting and exceeding our goals.

☐ Positive attitude.

☐ Taking on the tough jobs.

☐ Spirit of cooperation.

☐ Frankness and willingness to offer constructive advice and criticism.

☐ Courage to take risks.

☐ Self-sacrifice and generosity of spirit.

☐ Vision, creativity, and receptivity to new ideas.

☐ Common sense.

☐ Courtesy and sincerity.

☐ Trust and loyalty.

☐ Ability to really listen.

☐ Thoughtfulness and ability to help others.

☐ Ability to think and act strategically.

10

FIRING

The Role of the Leader

■ ■ ■

Part of being a boss is being able to accept people's rage.
It's most helpful for the person being fired if you can take
their rage in a calm, accepting, understanding way.

—*Paul Browde*

The termination of employment is a significant, potentially traumatic
event for the individuals concerned as well as the organization.
Whether the reason is to remove incompetents, to create a consequence for misconduct, to reinforce standards, or to punish violations
of ethics, as a leader you must be well acquainted with the criteria
required for the dismissal. You must understand who has the authority to approve the decision, what your legal responsibilities are, and
what the process is for executing the action. You should try to help
everyone within your organization understand that the right decision
was made for the right reasons—with the process being fair and just.

As a general rule, you should dismiss individuals who report
directly to you, and not delegate that task to a human resources
person or someone else (although the involvement of your human
resources people is often required by company policy). Your involvement in the firing of other key individuals will depend on the circumstances.

For criminal or serious administrative misconduct, violations of
ethics, or serious integrity issues, the act of firing may be swift and

clean. For substandard job performance, most organizations have established a process that calls for comprehensive counseling over a period of time, with inadequate progress demonstrated before the evidence will be sufficient for dismissal. Where organizations get into trouble is a lack of documented adequate counseling over time on the individual at risk. In other words, the time for you to become informed on the process for firing is not the day you want to dismiss someone.

Before making a final decision on the firing, it is imperative to have a legal or human resource expert review the case. You want the process to be clean, efficient, and in accordance with the standards of the organization. Also, the process must be able to withstand the scrutiny of other influencing organizations—like the union or perhaps public or other private interest groups. Be sure you understand all of the ramifications of the decision to terminate so you can be prepared to address any issues that arise.

A good leader should know how to proceed with a firing action. As noted above, most organizations have standardized procedures for review before an individual is fired. For your direct reports and other key personnel, it is your responsibility to counsel the individual, in order to explain clearly where his or her job performance has been substandard. You should also make clear suggestions on how to improve performance, with measurable criteria. If, after a period of time (usually a few months), the performance results still do not reach an acceptable level, you should consider removing the individual from the position. If you do not have the authority to make this decision, you should consult with the person who does before you take any action. Once the decision is made, you need to personally meet with the employee in question and inform him or her of the decision. If the counseling was done correctly by an engaged and informed leader, the action will not be a surprise to the person being removed.

For new supervisors (and even some seasoned professionals), this type of confrontation with a substandard employee is not easy. If you have never done this before, seek the counsel of those who have. Rehearsing the actual session with a friend or colleague may be useful. There is no question that every session having to do with counseling substandard performance will be a learning session. You will want to be firm and specific in your comments but will also want to demonstrate empathy and concern as appropriate.

If you have lost confidence in the employee's ability to do the job, you may wish to determine first how *the employee* thinks he or she is doing. If the employee thinks he or she has been doing great and you think otherwise, you really have to be prepared to outline how the individual has failed to meet the goals set. During this session, it is important for you to give the associate who is being removed the opportunity to explain what problems exist and how he or she feels about this action. Be patient and be a passive listener. It can be a very traumatic experience for an individual being fired.

You have a responsibility to help the employee work through this difficult experience. You will want to demonstrate genuine empathy for this person's position and talk at length to the individual about future prospects. If appropriate, you should offer to help in finding him or her a new position. You should explain that you will write a final evaluation that will ensure that the individual's strengths are outlined just as fairly as his or her weaknesses.

In some cases, the individual has failed so badly in performance, integrity, or some other area that you must be quite tough on the final performance appraisal report. If the employee is being fired for cause (not just for substandard performance, but for a gross violation of integrity or extremely poor performance), there should be no question remaining in that employee's mind—or in the final report—about why he or she is being fired.

When a firing occurs, you may need to share this news with others in the organization. People will want to know what happened and why. The anxiety generated by the action will not dissipate until you share the information with your key people. It is best if there is no delay in the getting the word out. Other employees will be watching how you manage the departure process. If you accomplish it ruthlessly and with little consideration for the individual's fellow workers who are affected, this action will have a negative impact on the morale of the organization.

Following a speech that Perry made on leadership to a health center, in which he made the point that there were a number of organizations that were tolerating too many incompetent employees, a middle manager confessed to him that "the toleration of incompetence is the cancer that is destroying our hospital."

Leaders who never fire anyone—or who move them out of positions in which they are underperforming despite their talents—may be doing a disservice to their institutions. Many people take advantage when they know that they are safe from the real discipline of being fired. Therefore, a deserved firing is not only the right thing to do, but also sets the tone that there are certain standards of performance and ethics that must be met. It is an important part of any leader's responsibility to fire the individuals who, after proper counseling, fail to live up to the organization's standards.

Termination Checklist

The difficult duty of firing an associate can be made somewhat easier if you undertake it systematically. Make sure you understand the correct process, your organization's policies, and the legal requirements.

- ☐ Seek expert advice from legal and human resources before the decision.

- ☐ Ensure that the process is being executed in accordance with your organization's standard policies.

- ☐ Ensure that the individual has been given proper counseling—and warning—with opportunities to improve.

- ☐ Determine who needs to know what *before* the actual firing action takes place.

- ☐ Determine what information needs to be shared with others in the organization after the dismissal.

- ☐ Outline reasons for the decision:

  - ☐ Loss of confidence in employee's abilities

  - ☐ Lack of adequate competence

  - ☐ Lack of ability to meet deadlines

  - ☐ Lack of integrity

  - ☐ Poor attitude

  - ☐ Chronic absenteeism

  - ☐ Inability to get along with boss/peers/subordinates

☐ Inability to keep up with rapidly changing technology

☐ Inability to establish good working relationships with customers and colleagues

☐ Ask what the employee might want to do next and how you can help.

☐ Ask what lessons can be drawn from this setback.

☐ Ask if there are any things about which you may not be aware, about the person's personal situation or concerning the organization. (Be a patient listener because the person may unload on you.)

☐ If appropriate (and if available according to your organization's policies), offer professional assistance—outplacement support, financial or legal advisors, counseling, etc.

☐ Explain what kind of evaluation report the individual can expect and to what extent, if any, you are willing to give references to prospective employers.

PART III

Leading Organizations

11

TAKING OVER

The Vital Nature of the Transition

■ ■ ■

Whenever you are asked if you can do a job, tell 'em, "Certainly I can!" Then get busy and find out how to do it.

—*Theodore Roosevelt*

Well begun is half done.

—*Aristotle*

Many individuals taking over leadership positions—or those in a position to advise them—do not think through the transition process. They fail to develop a "take charge" plan, and so they miss opportunities to be well prepared for their new responsibilities. By systematically approaching the transition process, a leader can be much more effective in those critical first few weeks in a new position. The transition process is particularly important for someone coming into a large or complex organization. Any executive about to assume the role of leader must deal not only with the requirements of the job but also with the personal psychological challenges that the transition presents, especially for those who have never run an organization before.

Few things can destroy the morale and health of a good organization more quickly than a new leader coming into the organization who makes significant decisions early on without first learning about the organization and soliciting advice from other high-ranking individuals who represent various parts of the organization. This arrogance clearly shows a lack of respect for the people and jeopardizes the trust needed for the new management structure to function fully and effectively. The environment created by this egotistical behavior can seldom be overcome, and thus begins the downward spiral.

As a new leader you need to ask critical questions—and get the answers from the best and most unbiased sources, preferably before officially taking over. In an ideal world you will have the opportunity to engage with the departing leader, from whom you can learn much. At the same time, you must be aware of the perspective from which this information is coming, since all leaders are susceptible to personal prejudices—and will try to protect those people and systems that they have supported and implemented during their tenure. Your goal should be to determine the concerns, problems, and frustrations that have occurred in the organization. You should seek a frank evaluation of the major personnel to determine who will be invaluable to you in the short and the long run, who may need to be reassigned or need counseling, and who may not, in the long term, contribute to the ongoing health and success of the organization.

While you may prefer not to receive the departing leader's evaluations of the various strengths and weaknesses of associates, you may then find yourself playing the leadership game with a partial deck of cards, and you can make major mistakes that could do great harm to the organization. Knowledge of the strengths and weaknesses of key personnel as you assume your leadership position should be as complete as possible.

When feasible, you should seek to have a number of transition questions answered before assuming new responsibilities—if not by the departing head then by a top assistant or key individuals within the organization. Many of the answers will be found in documents within the company—internal and external reports, performance evaluations, and other human resources information, financial state-

ments, etc. However, many of the answers to these quesʮʮʮʮ.
have to be found outside the organization—from independent reports,
annual statements, analysts, and other reliable sources. The most
important questions to ask are:

What is the mission?

What is the vision?

What are the organization's desired outputs?

What is the strategic plan?

What goals have been established?

What are the priorities?

What is the financial situation?

What Are the Organization's Standards of Integrity?

Any organization's reputation can be discovered in a number of
ways. Media reports can be helpful. You can also learn from those
who have worked there in the past or those who follow the company's
operations (customers, clients, vendors, and so on). Even prior to inter-
viewing for a position, you should do your homework to determine
if there are issues that may surface during your tenure that need to
be addressed immediately.

Most organizations have a code of ethics that all employees are
required to read and acknowledge. If such a document does not exist,
it may be a telling sign that needs to be remedied, and quickly. Every
organization, however big or small, should codify the conduct by which
it and its employees act. It is essential that you identify the organization's standards of integrity and feel confident that everyone is following those standards. Review the reporting and inspection systems
to ensure that they reinforce, rather than undermine, integrity. Be

sure that there is an ombudsman, or an inspector general, whom anyone with an ethical concern can approach without penalty. Without constant nurturing, high ethical standards can rapidly deteriorate.

What Is the Current Morale?

In addition to the big-picture issues, the specifics are equally important. It is essential to gain a thorough understanding of the operation of the whole organization and your place in it.

As you visit the various parts of your new organization, be sure to ask open-ended questions. "How is it going?" "What's happening?" "How is your day going?" "Do you have any problems I can help you with?" This approach will help you get a sense of the state of the morale of both individuals and the organization as a whole. If you notice a general feeling of joy or of gloom, you will be on course to determine the morale of those you will lead.

How Do I Compare to My Predecessor?

You will gain valuable knowledge by taking an objective look at the individual you are replacing. If the organization is in great shape and your predecessor has been a popular leader, it may be worthwhile to continue past policies, to let everybody know that you are honored to follow someone of such stature, and to articulate your hope that you will be able to keep the performance and morale at high levels. If the individual was very popular but the performance of the organization has been fairly low, you have a greater challenge. You must be willing to demand higher performance levels without denigrating the previous leader. If you are following an individual who was very cold, harsh, or unpopular, but the organization has been functioning well, then your task is easy. By reaching out to people, by thanking and complimenting them often, and by being approachable, you can lift performance even higher by enhancing morale.

Is There Anything That, If Made Public, Could Embarrass My Predecessor or Me?

Are there festering problems that are just waiting to jump up and bite me? In other words, are there "skeletons" and, if so, in what "closet"? It is important to ascertain if there are key individuals in the organization who have serious health problems, including alcoholism, drug abuse, and psychiatric difficulties. Research whether the reporting procedures for harassment are working and working well. Furthermore, confirm that women and minority groups trust these procedures and the people to whom problems would be reported. It is useful to root out institutional "skeletons in the closet" that may not have been revealed in normal reporting for fear that the organization or the boss would look bad, or that corporate credibility would suffer.

Who Is My Boss and What Are His or Her Expectations for Me and for the Organization?

Since the person to whom you report was likely involved in the hiring process, you may have (in fact, should have) an understanding of your employer's expectations for you and for the organization. But in a job interview, you may not have gained a sense of your superior's satisfactions and dissatisfactions with the organization. The earlier you have these forthright conversations the better. Even if your boss feels the organization is doing fine, there is always room for improvement and you will want to determine how these improvements can be made and how long they will take. These discussions, which will inevitably be ongoing, will lead to some very useful insights concerning both the organization and your boss, including his or her understanding of the problems of organizational rejuvenation. You should also meet with the key associates who work for your boss, in order to get their views of the strengths and problem areas within your new organization.

What Groups Will I Be Serving, Either Directly or Indirectly?

Leaders normally have to serve many constituencies, including shareholders, the board of directors, employees, customers, subcontractors, retired executives and associates, interest groups, and alumni. It is useful to determine who best represents the interests of these constituencies and with whom to meet. As you assume a leadership position, you are automatically assigned an essential role within a communication network. It is vital that you understand that network—both its formal and informal components.

Who Will Report Directly to Me?

The careful reading of personnel records, as well as discussions with your predecessor and your superior, will help you assess the qualifications of your associates and the scope of your duties. An experienced personnel or human resources director is another important source of information. But nothing will be as effective as one-on-one interviews with your direct reports as soon as possible after you take charge.

It is useful to find out if subordinate leaders have regular counseling sessions with the people who work under them and if poor performance is being identified, documented, and corrected.

To ensure the continuity of the organization over the next few years, you should look at projections and plans and how personnel fit into these. You will have to consider a range of circumstances, from scheduled retirements to anticipating departures of key subordinates, to establishing a promotion system that will give younger employees opportunities for upward mobility.

What Is the Overall Size and Structure of the Organization That I Am About to Lead?

Is the present organizational structure effective, and is it, at the same time, encouraging initiative and innovation? You need to dig into issues of organizational effectiveness to ensure that there is a workable span of control without too many people reporting directly to the leader. As you examine the structural setup, become aware not only of the present effect on productivity, but also of potential effects to come. Initiative and innovation must be tapped, for they will determine the future success of the organization. You may need to implement changes to the organizational structure that will allow for positive change to occur.

Many large organizations have geographically separated plants, divisions, bureaus, or units that report to a top leader either directly or indirectly. You not only should be fully aware of your responsibilities to each of these sites, but also should find out how best to communicate with each one. Neglecting field operations is a common leadership problem. It is easy for the leader to get caught up in a combination of corporate business matters at headquarters and in various outreach responsibilities. Spending a significant amount of time with field organizations allows you as a leader to learn, first-hand, the challenges and successes of these parts of the company; to demonstrate your involvement, interest, and respect; and to communicate your policy, plans, and concerns more directly than any memo could accomplish.

Are the Performance Standards of the Organization Being Met?

It is reasonably easy to ascertain whether deadlines are being met, if products are of high quality, and if overall performance is acceptable. You should look carefully at the performance records of subordinate organizations and staff agencies to ensure that standards are being met and, when they are not, that prompt, appropriate action is taken.

You should spend considerable time reading the reports of (and talking to) auditors, inspectors, and evaluators. It is quite c to find that an organization has an inflated view of its own performance—and occasionally the opposite. It is importa into a job with an objective understanding of both the perceptions and the realities. For the conscientious leader, this process of assessment is ongoing.

Finally, if you take over an organization that is not attaining expected results, you have a unique opportunity to communicate that it is time for everyone in the organization to chart a new course, to recognize the deficiencies that have been preventing optimal achievement, and to work together to upgrade performance at all levels.

What Are the Various Means of Communication Available That I Can Use to Interact with My Associates?

Many large organizations publish newspapers or newsletters on a regular basis. These publications give you the opportunity to write a column on a subject that you want to share with your people. Also, local radio and television stations are marvelous avenues through which you can reach out to the members of your team and their families. Corporate DVDs, email, staff meetings, trips to subordinate organizations, and speeches to various groups are a few more ways in which the active leader can communicate effectively with associates.

To be an effective leader, you must work hard to avoid "groupthink"—a situation in which there is too much compatibility and a consensus is found too quickly. False consensus, excessive conformity, and groupthink are bad for any organization. Even though some of the concerns raised by associates may be parochial or ill-conceived, the leader must be willing to listen carefully before a final decision is made. There is a direct relationship between the thoroughness and openness of the decision-making process and the effectiveness of the implementation process. If associates are given a full opportunity to express their views prior to your making the decision, they will be more willing to carry out the decision after it is made, even though it may not be the one that they would have chosen.

Going Forward

After you have been in charge for two or three months, write a "state of the company" or "state of the department" letter. Using your own words, state the goals and priorities of the organization, as well as particular points that are important to you. This letter can let everyone know that you have a good grasp of the organization, have established clear and understandable goals, and have laid out areas of concentration. The letter, in draft form, should be circulated among key associates for comments and criticism. It is important that they be comfortable with the letter, since they will be responsible for supporting both the goals and the underlying philosophy. The contents should be summarized in the company, university, or post newspaper, and the letter itself should be widely circulated both in hard copy and by email. It should be given to all new employees so that they can understand and identify with both the organization and the leader.

Even if you are not the CEO (or ultimate head of an organization), as a middle manager or division chief you will find this exercise equally valuable. It can be adapted to your unique circumstance and shared not only with your associates but, of equal importance, with those to whom you report.

The letter should be brief (no more than two pages), upbeat, and nonthreatening. It should clearly reflect your thoughts and dreams for the organization. Specific points that may be useful to highlight in the philosophy letter include:

- The rich and successful history of the organization

- The commitment to internal and community goals

- The need for high personal and institutional integrity

- The vision of the leader and the organization

- The policy of decentralization and empowerment of subordinate leaders

- The seeking of diversity

- The need for innovation

- The process whereby creative ideas are advanced

By committing to write this letter within three months of taking over, you make the important step from being the "new boss" to being the person fully in charge. After you have been in charge for about a year, review the letter, revise it, and rewrite it as necessary to reflect any changes in your vision, goals, and philosophy of leadership. (A professionally produced DVD can also be a powerful way to communicate. Like the letter, it should be short—ten minutes or less.)

You should not underestimate the advantages of a well-planned transition into leadership. If you take on the transition process carefully and systematically, you can quickly get the attention and respect of coworkers. A successful transition can make a big difference in both the future performance and the self-esteem of the organization. If you create an atmosphere that encourages and validates high integrity, planning, and open communication, the organization soon can become a model for others to emulate.

12

Mission, Vision, and Values

Establishing the Foundation for

Successful Organizations

■ ■ ■

Good business leaders create a vision, articulate the vision, passionately own the vision, and relentlessly drive it to completion.

—*Jack Welch*

Setting the foundation for success in any organization begins with the development of the mission, the vision, and the values. Addressing these three objectives will help you serve the long-term interests of your institution. While each of these tasks has a unique purpose, they are related and need to be in step with one another. Without them organizations have no destination, direction, standards, or bounds within which to operate. On occasion, successful organizations combine the vision with the mission, but in doing so they still address each of the three objectives.

Leaders who care about their mission and about their people normally desire to leave their organizations in better shape and with a clearer direction than when they took over. Well-defined missions, visions, and values should be folded into a strategic plan (see Chapter 13, "Creating a Strategic Plan"). Once established, your role as the leader is to bring them to life. The rigorous execution of a meet challenges and pursue opportunities will drive the orga

...er levels of sustained performance and an enviable legacy for
...s leader.

The Mission

An organization's mission statement should affirm the *purpose* of
the organization—why the organization exists, what *it does every
day*. It is a simple statement, described with action words, and may
include measurable objectives. It is written for the benefit of the
members of the organization, stockholders, and stakeholders.

Decisions and priorities should be based on the mission. Every
member of your organization should understand his or her contribution to the mission, with recognition and rewards programs in place
to help everyone stay focused. Ultimately, the success of any organization is measured not by how hard people try but rather by the
successful accomplishment of the stated goals that contribute to the
accomplishment of the mission. Abraham Lincoln's personal mission
was to "preserve the Union." Nelson Mandela made his life's mission
to "end apartheid," and Mother Teresa's personal mission was to
"show mercy and compassion for the dying." Each of these was a
powerful personal mission statement exemplifying a simple, focused
cause.

Mission statements evolve over time and as leadership changes.
The following are fine examples of mission statements from successful companies, past and present:

Ford Motor Company: We are a global family with a proud heritage
passionately committed to providing personal mobility for people
around the world.

Procter & Gamble: We will provide branded products and services
of superior quality and value that improve the lives of the world

consumers. As a result, consumers will reward us with leadership sales, profit, and value creation, allowing our shareholders and the communities in which we live and work to prosper.

Morgan Stanley: To deliver the finest financial thinking, products, and execution in the world.

Microsoft: To be the world's #1 provider of innovative technology solutions that help realize the full potential of diverse customers and partners around the world.

Apple: Committed to bringing the best personal computing experience to students, educators, creative professionals, and consumers around the world through innovative hardware, software, and Internet offerings.

Walt Disney Company: We create happiness by providing the finest in entertainment for people of all ages, everywhere.

U.S. Military Academy: To educate, train, and inspire the Corps of Cadets so that each graduate is a commissioned leader of character committed to the values of Duty, Honor, Country, and prepared for a career of professional excellence and service to the Nation as an officer in the U.S. Army.

The Augusta Museum of History: To collect, preserve, and interpret history in relation to the past of Augusta and the Central Savannah River Region for education and enrichment of present and future generations.

ConocoPhillips: To use our pioneering spirit to responsibly deliver energy to the world.

Google: To organize the world's information and make it universally accessible and useful.

Nike Inc.: To bring inspiration and innovation to every athlete in the world.

U.S. Air Force: To fly, fight, and win . . . in air, space, and cyber-space.

Each one of these mission statements is short and easy to understand. Mission statements that are too wordy are generally the result of a committee effort where each of the members inserts ideas that he or she deems to be important. While the team may have input on the mission statement, in the end it is leader who must decide what is included and why.

The Vision

A vision describes the purpose of an organization in terms of values and the future—what the organization wants to be. It should be a source of inspiration—what you will achieve because you will execute the mission so exceedingly well. The target audience includes the members of the organization plus those outside the organization who want to know why they should invest or work with the organization.

The adage "If you don't know where you are going, any path will get you there" should be a reminder that without a well-defined and well-understood vision, an organization is likely to flounder. The vision should be clear and succinct as it focuses the organization on its most important long-range goals and priorities. (And it must be in sync with your parent organization if you have one.)

Just as you want a keynote speaker at a conference to "light up the room" and inspire every member of the audience, your vision statement should also shoot high. It should not be just a repetition or an embellishment of your mission statement.

Developing this vision statement for your organization can be an enriching experience. The process itself provides an organization the opportunity to develop teams and teamwork. In order for your people to feel a sense of ownership in the vision statement, and to help foster creative thinking among your subordinate leaders, you need to allocate time for the team to meet and discuss the various options that will lead to the creation of the vision statement.

According to Laurie Beth Jones, speaker and bestselling author of *Jesus CEO*: "A vision statement is an exercise in visualization. A vision statement requires a company to write down exactly what the 'picture' will look like once the mission has been carried out.

"It is best," she continues, "if you place the mission and vision statements side by side. Many television sets will allow you to watch two football games simultaneously. [Similarly, you should] watch channel WCI (What Currently Is) and channel WCB (What Could Be). Keeping these two pictures present allows for you, your team, and your company to align the mission seamlessly with the vision."

Like mission statements, vision statements change over time as organizations change. Some examples of meaningful vision statements have included:

Ford Motor Company: To become the world's leading Consumer Company for automotive products and services.

Procter & Gamble: Be and be recognized as the best consumer products and services company in the world.

Morgan Stanley: Connecting people, ideas, and capital, we will be our clients' first choice for achieving their financial aspirations.

Microsoft: To be led by a globally diverse workforce that consistently delivers outstanding business results, understands the various cultural demands of a global marketplace, is passionate about technology and the promise it holds to tap human potential, and thrives in a corporate culture where inclusive behaviors are valued.

Apple: To make a contribution to the world by making tools for the mind that advance humankind.

Ken Blanchard Companies: To be the number one advocate in the world for human worth in organizations.

U.S. Air Force: Global Vigilance, Reach, and Power: A vision that orbits around three core competencies: developing airmen, technology to war fighting, and integrating operations. These core competencies make our six distinctive capabilities possible: air and space superiority, global attack, rapid global mobility, precision engagement, information superiority, and agile combat support.

Values

Values of an organization help define its culture and act as guiding principles for influencing thoughts and behaviors. When values are established, communicated, and accepted by the members of an organization, they help create an environment that fosters cohesion and esprit. They define the character of the organization. Values help the decision-making process of an organization, especially if leaders make adherence to these values a priority.

To be most effective, values should be developed and validated by key members of the organization themselves, ensuring a high degree of buy-in. They must be well known, well documented, well understood, and frequently broadcast throughout the organization.

Stakeholders (employees, stock holders, customers, vendors) know what the organization stands for and what defines acceptable behavior and beliefs.

In crafting a values statement for your organization, consider the following. Be inspired by the ideas listed below, set your own priorities, and add to this list as you feel appropriate:

The Boy Scouts of America: A Scout is trustworthy, loyal, helpful, friendly, courteous, kind, obedient, cheerful, thrifty, brave, clean, and reverent.

Walt Disney Company: (1) No cynicism, (2) Nurturing and promulgation of "wholesome American values," (3) Creativity, dreams, and imagination, (4) Fanatical attention to consistency and detail, and (5) Preservation and control of the Disney "magic."

Ken Blanchard Companies: (1) Ethical behavior, (2) Relationships, (3) Success, (4) Learning.

U.S. Army: Loyalty, duty, respect, selfless service, honor, integrity, and personal courage.

U.S. Marine Corps: The motto *Semper Fi* (short for *Semper Fidelis*) means "forever faithful." All Marines are expected to have loyalty to "Corps and Country" and to their fellow fighting men and women, for the rest of their days.

A Statement of Values

Johnson & Johnson is a global company that embraces a vision to commit to "research and science—bringing innovative ideas, products and services to advance the health and well-being of people." J&J publishes a credo that spells out the values that guide their decision-making and that embodies its mission. In the company's own words, the credo "challenges [us] to put the needs and well-being of the people [we] serve *first* . . . It is more than just a moral compass. We believe it's a recipe for business success."

Johnson & Johnson's Credo

We believe our first responsibility is to the doctors, nurses and patients, to mothers and fathers and all others who use our products and services. In meeting their needs everything we do must be of high quality. We must constantly strive to reduce our costs in order to maintain reasonable prices. Customers' orders must be serviced promptly and accurately. Our suppliers and distributors must have an opportunity to make a fair profit.

We are responsible to our employees, the men and women who work with us throughout the world. Everyone must be considered as an individual. We must respect their dignity and recognize their merit. They must have a sense of security in their jobs. Compensation must be fair and adequate, and working conditions clean, orderly and safe. We must be mindful of ways to help our employees fulfill their family responsibilities. Employees must feel free to make suggestions and complaints. There must be equal opportunity for employment, development and advancement for those qualified. We must provide competent management, and their actions must be just and ethical.

We are responsible to the communities in which we live and work and to the world community as well. We must be good citizens: support good works and charities and bear our fair share of taxes. We must encourage civic improvements and better health and education. We must maintain in good order the property we are privileged to use, protecting the environment and natural resources.

Our final responsibility is to our stockholders. Business must make a sound profit.

We must experiment with new ideas. Research must be carried on, innovative programs developed and mistakes paid for. New equipment must be purchased, new facilities provided and new products launched. Reserves must be created to provide for adverse times. When we operate according to these principles, the stockholders should realize a fair return.

When mission, vision, and values are well defined, effectively communicated to all, and well integrated into the strategic plans, they can lead to monumental success of an organization, as evidenced by the organizations represented in this chapter and many more. Together, these elements provide the foundation for establishing the organization's culture—the key to success in building a successful enterprise. Leader development programs are essential in establishing and sustaining this culture throughout the workforce. As a leader, you will serve your organization well by pursuing these critical tasks and setting the foundation for success.

13

CREATING A STRATEGIC PLAN

A Road Map to Success

■ ■ ■

Long range planning does not deal with future decisions,
but with the future of present decisions.

—*Peter F. Drucker*

If you don't know where you are going, you are certain to
end up somewhere else.

—*Yogi Berra*

The strategic plan articulates where you want your organization to
go and how you plan to get there. Once you have established the
mission and vision, and everyone understands the underlying values
that inform everything that you do, the next critical task is to develop
and execute a strategic plan. To be among the best leaders, you have
to be not only a visionary and a decision-maker, but also an expert
planner. If you decide that planning is not your strong suit, it's essential that you hire the right person to lead this important effort.

When you take charge, especially of a large organization, two of
the most important questions you should ask yourself are: "What is
the strategic plan?" and "Who are the strategic planners?" If you
are not committed to an institutionalized planning process, you will
likely become merely a caretaker who is unable to raise the organization to higher levels of performance.

> **A mind stretched by a new idea never returns to its**
> **original dimension.**
> —ABRAHAM LINCOLN

Why a Strategic Plan?

A strategic plan helps establish intentional order in a potentially chaotic situation. Such a plan forces you to look into and search for opportunities to influence the future. The well-developed plan helps organizations to define success and establish achievable, measurable goals. A considered plan promotes the establishment of priorities and guides the investment of finite resources within the organization. The plan provides the framework to build a system of accountability as well as a sense of direction and continuity for the organization. Over time, a plan that is clear and specific yet realistic and flexible will provide a mechanism of review for you to stay within the field of your organization's expertise and not run into trouble.

The process of developing the plan must be transparent so all have the opportunity to watch, understand what is happening, and offer feedback.

This procedure is a valuable team-building event—perhaps as important as the end product itself. Every member of your workforce wants to know how he or she fits into the present situation and to be recognized as a contributor to the future success. A comprehensive plan takes every person's role into account. But if there are people who do not see themselves anywhere in the plan, you need to resolve that situation by making sure that either the mission is modified or the employee is re-tasked to a different part of the mission.

One major goal of a planning system is to encourage creativity and innovation throughout the organization. Many leaders give lip service to innovation while failing to create either the climate or the organizational structure to encourage it. Periodically, leaders should examine the quality, quantity, and velocity of innovation within their organizations. They should be open to new ideas while being sensitive to the turbulence that the implementation of new ideas can often cause. Including this message in a strategic plan will establish the tone of your leadership.

Finally, the existence of and adherence to a plan can be seen as an effective tool for engaging stakeholders and other influencers who may be interested in serving or contributing to the organization.

The bottom line is that the plan helps you gain control of the future and the destiny of your organization.

7 Keys to Crafting a Successful Plan

1. Choose the Best Team to Draft the Plan

No CEO writes the strategic plan alone. Draw on the most talented and experienced people from throughout the organization (or from a pool of consultants) for this purpose. Successful CEOs don't assume that just because they can run one division or another successfully, they can run anything and everything equally well. (See Chapter 1, "Becoming Self-Aware: The Importance of Introspection.") Since individuals within the organization often view planning from very different perspectives, you must understand that planning in the budget office is quite different from planning in the operational divisions, or in the personnel or marketing directorates. It is the task of the leader to establish a system that allows specialized planning to take place, but always within the context of a cohesive strategic planning system.

An effective team will act as both a clearinghouse for and innovator of ideas. Equally important, the team will be able to communicate effectively—in writing or personal presentations.

2. Clarify Your Expectations

Since you will be asking a team of people to develop a workable plan, you have to be prepared to guide and advise them during this process. You have to be very clear about the intentions of the strategic plan, reinforce the mission and vision of the organization, and provide the parameters and deadlines in which the team will work. You and your top leaders guiding this process have to do your homework, know what you want and need to achieve, and have a fairly firm grasp on how to get it done. If you are a new leader, stakeholders from within and outside the company will be watching—and they will not be prepared to wait too long before you present your ideas.

3. Keep the Planning Process on Course

To ensure that the development of the plan does not get bogged down, you and your top leaders must have direct access to the planning team and should schedule regular meetings with them in order to:

• Clarify the intention of the plan.

• Facilitate decision-making on the content and organization.

• Present outlines or drafts for review.

• Discuss sensitive issues that are not appropriate for more open forums.

Designated individuals from the team should also have access on an ad hoc basis to you or other decision-makers throughout the entire process, particularly when critical issues arise that may create roadblocks for the planners.

4. Be Flexible

Just as each division of your organization will have its own requirements and priorities for the plan, you have to be prepared to accommodate both these needs and the changing landscape. Current events, business developments, catastrophic occurrences, changes in personnel, or even acts of nature may threaten to undo the best laid plan. You have to allow for these contingencies not only during the development stages of the plan but also once it has been written and implemented. In fact, allowances for these contingencies need to be built into every plan.

5. Determine the Plan's Duration

The length of time that the plan covers will be dependent on the type of organization and its mission. In the fast-paced environment of today's business world, projections—especially when it comes to the details of execution—beyond eighteen to twenty-four months may stretch credibility. For certain industries, such as manufacturing facilities where long lead times and significant expenses are tied to major modifications to the facility, a plan for three to five years may be more appropriate. Many organizations may wish to keep shorter-range plans within a budget cycle or tailor the duration to specific circumstances of the organization, the marketplace, or the expectations of owners and shareholders. Those same owners and shareholders will want to see action sooner than later but will be assured if they are presented with a workable and reasonable plan.

6. Decide What the Plan Will Include and How It Will Be Organized

A superior strategic plan must not only include the most essential elements of what and how the business will be run but also be presented in a straightforward, easy-to-understand, and logical way. The organization of the content will depend on the message that you want to deliver, and you may choose to present the components chronologically or from big picture to detail. Whichever organizational method you choose, be consistent to avoid confusion and repetition.

Regardless of your approach, typically you will include most or all of the following:

- The mission and vision: Accomplishing the mission and fulfilling the vision is the fundamental purpose of the plan.

- Assessment of the current environment: Identify and articulate the organization's strengths and weaknesses as well at the opportunities and threats (SWOT).

- Primary and subordinate goals: Presented in logically organized groups, these goals must help simplify the complex mission and clarify and reinforce the vision. They will indicate priorities that will facilitate implementation of actions for short- *and* long-term wins for the organization.

- Action items: Articulate as clearly and concisely as possible what needs to be done in the short, mid, or long term.

- Personnel: Designate which group/division/person will be responsible for *implementation* of the respective actions. Identify—by name, title, and/or division—the right people with the right skills and experience to lead these efforts.

- Always learning: One of the most important elements of your strategic plan should focus on the development and retention of your people. Just as there are technical skills required by many, there are discrete leadership skills that are required by some. Identifying those needs and investing in continuing education and leadership development programs are vital line items in your strategic plan.

- Metrics for measuring progress: As management guru Peter Drucker said, "If you can't measure it, you can't manage it." At regular intervals, every stakeholder in your organization will want and need to know how well (or poorly) the organization is performing in order to take steps to maximize the potential and/or remedy problems.

7. Be Succinct

Brevity is not only the soul of wit; it is the hallmark of a good strategic plan. A few words chosen wisely will give you the best result. The ideal strategic plan should be as brief as you can make it without losing inclusion of the essential components. The length will vary, depending on the size and complexity of your organization—and the ambitions that you have for the short and long term. Since the object of the plan is to provide a *framework* for the direction of your organization, much of the detail as to how you will accomplish the goals you set forth can be left to future discussion or more specific review with those who will be directly involved with these activities.

Of equal importance is the fact that you want to encourage every stakeholder to familiarize him- or herself with this document and, in practical terms, the longer the chronicle, the lower the readership. As well, you want to engage everyone in the process, and an over-abundance of detail may discourage readers from offering input or rob them of the confidence that they can put the parts of the plan for which they are responsible into effect. (The sign of a good leader is allowing people the scope to innovate and solve problems without being restricted by bureaucratic protocols and arbitrary proscriptions.)

Any plan can be supplemented with appendices or classified supplements that cover detail—sensitive technologies, concepts in development, or pending actions—that you may not wish to see so widely disseminated and that can be circulated at your discretion on a need-to-know basis.

Look to the Future

> I am interested in the future because that's where I plan
> to spend the rest of my life.
> —VARIOUSLY ATTRIBUTED TO CHARLES F. KETTERING,
> CHARLIE CHAPLIN, WOODY ALLEN, GEORGE BURNS, AND
> BUCKMINSTER FULLER, AMONG OTHERS

While your strategic plan may cover the next eighteen to twenty-four months, or longer in certain cases, a good plan needs to anticipate both the natural evolution of an organization and the unexpected turn of events, as indicated above in the section called "Be Flexible." It is a critical task to implement changes an organization needs to maintain its relevance or profitability in the marketplace. Two aspects of corporate development that are keys to the organization's health, especially for any large or global group, are divestitures and acquisitions. Both merit a brief discussion here and inclusion in your strategic plan.

All large organizations need to pursue aggressive divestiture strategies to ensure that they do not retain outdated or antiquated policies, offices, doctrines, or research and development programs. Likewise, organizations need to pursue acquisition strategies when opportunities present themselves. Economic analysis in a profit-making firm normally points to areas of weakness and obsolescence within the organization but can also highlight where an opportunity exists that merits exploration for possible expansion. In government, divestiture is a more challenging process because outmoded areas are harder to identify and more difficult to exorcise from the organization.

Technical competence in an organization's major endeavors is an important attribute without which the likelihood of failure increases. Hence, divestiture is not just unloading the "dogs," it is also selling off the parts of the business that do not fit within the corporate "essence" or play to its strengths. In the postwar U.S. military, for example, General George Marshall was very wise to support an autonomous, separate U.S. Air Force so that the Army could concentrate its strength where its competency was highest: ground combat.

George Marshall's commitment to planning, his knowledge of where the truly talented and innovative young professionals were, and his willingness to hire, nurture, and reward them played a vital role in the success of the United States during World War II. The dynamic planning that was done just prior to World War II helped ensure the achievements of the Army and the Army Air Corps. Marshall's commitment to creativity played an important role in the establishment of a separate Air Force, the development of the Marshall Plan, and the significant strategic planning efforts in the War and State Departments in the 1940s. As both a military and civilian government leader, Marshall was absolutely superb—without peer in his time—in creating an atmosphere of high integrity, trust, creativity, and a sense of mission in all the organizations he led: the U. S. Army, the Department of State, and the Department of Defense. If you are looking for a model after whom to pattern yourself, George Marshall would be our recommendation.

Another marvelous example of leadership in demonstrating the need for strategic planning was General Hap Arnold. By the summer of 1943, he had created a planning division that focused its full attention on the challenges and opportunities of the post-war world. He also created the RAND Corporation shortly after World War II. This was an important and innovative step. RAND soon became a model research agency where high-quality, policy-relevant, and, most important, interdisciplinary research was accomplished. The creation of RAND and its impact on planning and policy-making in the Air Force is historically unique. It set the pattern for many similar research groups that support governmental organizations or institutions.

Keys to Successful Implementation of the Plan

There may be some resistance within the organization to the process of codifying a plan, and you need to be sensitive to this probability. One example is those who had bad experiences in the past wasting enormous time developing a plan only to see the plan sit on the shelf and never referenced again.

Another common issue is that priorities established in the plan are ignored as finite resources are regularly allocated elsewhere without any known justification—thereby jeopardizing the credibility of the plan and the leadership. Know the concerns of the people and address them early—the entire organization will benefit for the collaboration.

For any strategic plan to be successful, it must be credible. It must enjoy the full commitment of the organization's leaders and stakeholders. It requires a built-in mechanism for accountability. Consider the following as a vital checklist of questions for the successful implementation of your strategic plan:

- Has the plan been drafted in a clear and concise way that is accessible to all stakeholders?

- Does the plan support the organization's mission and vision?

- Is the plan doable?

- Have you identified those aspects of the plan that may be particularly challenging?

- Does the plan enjoy the buy-in of the organization, top to bottom?

- Do those who are "invested" in the process have a feeling of ownership?

- Is the plan linked to a parent organization where applicable?

• Does the plan clearly express both the message of and the metrics for each objective?

• Is there an established system of accountability so everyone knows what his or her role is in the execution of the plan?

• Is there a system that tracks the progress of the implementation and includes regular reviews of the major points of the plan and periodic reporting to present status and progress by those leaders accountable for each goal?

• Has clearly written, ongoing documentation of the status of the plan's implementation been made available to all designated stakeholders?

• Is the plan flexible, within reason, so that it can be adapted as circumstances warrant? Have you accounted for both predictable and unpredictable future events?

• Is there a process to address the failure to meet goals and to find and implement solutions in concert not only with the leaders who are accountable but with the group as a whole?

When Jeff took over as the commander of the U.S. Army Signal Center Headquarters, it was an organization faced with future reductions in resources with limited strategic direction and no well-defined priorities consistent with the Army's evolving plan for the future. The Signal Center is the home of the communications and information technology branch of the Army, where doctrine is developed, the strategic planning for future communications capabilities occurs, and where professional education, training, and leader development programs are designed and executed for the sixty thousand communications and computer operations personnel in the Active, National Guard, and Reserve Army. It was in critical need of a strategic plan.

Over a period of six months Jeff led the process that resulted in establishment of a refined vision and mission and the delineation of 8 major goals and 117 specific tasks to be accomplished over the next eighteen months. All of this was accomplished by following the keys to crafting and implementing a successful plan outlined in this chapter. Jeff and his team prepared and distributed throughout the Army a twelve-page "Executive Summary" to help market the strategic plan and inform all the stakeholders of the ongoing priorities of the Signal Headquarters. Over the next eighteen months, they implemented a process where every three months those leaders responsible for each of the goals presented their progress to the leadership group for assessment and discussion. The process was very transparent as important guiding principles were disseminated and decisions made. The quality of the plan, the buy-in by the leadership and the workforce, and the rigorous implementation of the process to hold people accountable for their tasks led to a far greater level of successful achievement.

When your vision is based on careful thought and research, you can lead the organization to new heights of performance and effectiveness. A strategic plan is the way to realize that vision and fulfill your mission. Conversely, if you reject planning, you will inevitably miss opportunities for growth and success. A combination of good systematic planning and flexible "adhocracy" can lead to extraordinary results.

14

DECENTRALIZING AND GETTING FEEDBACK

A Twin Dilemma

■   ■   ■

> Strange as it sounds, great leaders gain authority by giving it away.
>
> —*James Stockdale*

> It does an organization no good when its leader refuses to share his leadership function with his lieutenants. The more centers of leadership you find in a company, the stronger it will become.
>
> —*David Ogilvy*

There is a great deal of discussion in the literature on leadership that pertains to centralization versus decentralization. Most well-run organizations have balanced the two. At each level, there should be a certain amount of decision-making authority and a certain amount of empowerment. The best leaders have a solid grasp of every level of decision-making and authority. They know which decisions should be made at each level. In addition, they compliment subordinate leaders and associates for ensuring that decisions are being made at the appropriate levels. An essential element of the decentralization and delegating process is making sure that associates understand the organizational values, goals, priorities, and the "big picture." This is an ongoing endeavor with leaders at each level playing an important role as teachers who emphasize and reinforce the organization's standards. Decentralization and delegation do not mean that the senior leaders become invisible or disengaged; they signify that the hand on the tiller is a light one.

It is important for associates at all levels to receive psychological rewards for the work they do. This can be accomplished through trust in their authority and their decisions. Subordinate leaders should feel responsible and important. With the general trend in America toward better communication and more centralization, all leaders must work tirelessly to push decisions down to the appropriate levels.

A dilemma emerges as a direct result of the sophisticated network of communication and the diversity of feedback mechanisms that exist in large modern organizations. The following situation often occurs: A new leader takes over, reorganizes to enhance decentralization, articulates a philosophy of the empowerment of subordinate leaders, and establishes some excellent feedback mechanisms. As the feedback loops give the leader lots of information, he or she tends to jump into problem areas or areas of personal interest. Soon the leader is aggressively recentralizing the organization so that he or she can make decisions that subordinate leaders should be making.

How can you strike the proper balance between centralization and decentralization? Learn to accept feedback graciously—do not panic. Use the information to stay in touch with employees' concerns and ideas. Thus, you can be helpfully aware of, but not fully engaged in, decisions at every level. Also, help accomplish your goals by asking your subordinate leaders some key questions. Do not spend time struggling to resolve matters that competent associates can handle. On rare occasions, you may feel that you must jump into an issue or problem personally. When you do decide to get directly involved, you need to work closely with the subordinate leaders who normally have responsibility for this area. Thus, they will not feel disregarded, and they will gain valuable skills for the future. As a leader, you should stay in touch and stay involved but discipline any tendencies you have to be a "control freak" or you will slide down the slippery slope of continuous micromanagement. It is important to realize that micromanagement—the compulsive inclination to get personally involved in an infinite number of unimportant details—is seldom productive for leaders.

In an organization that has the proper amount of decentralization, the leader must ensure that there are a number of effective feedback mechanisms. The normal hierarchical structure (or chain of command in the military) that often provides excellent feedback is helpful, but other means are needed to supplement it. An inspection system and an auditing system are two methods by which you can obtain essential information. You should have a close relationship with both the chief inspector and the auditor. It is important for them to tell you the whole and unvarnished truth. The inspection system must be staffed with excellent people who, because of their recognized competence, have the respect of individuals at all levels. This inspection system must emphasize integrity and not deteriorate into a pattern of activity that permits the withholding of important information. Self-inspection systems within subordinate organizations also can be effective tools. You should show interest in and support for such systems and ask for periodic reports on problem areas uncovered by self-inspection.

Management control systems, which allow a great deal of quantifiable data to reach the leader, are also useful feedback mechanisms. However, in their worst forms, they can become heavy burdens, detract from the mission, and deteriorate into data manipulation and dishonest reporting. Do not take for granted that computer access to all kinds of information within the organization is timely or accurate. If the information in the computer system is found to be inaccurate or dishonest, you should take corrective action or, if necessary, shut down the system. The information flow must be restored so that it effectively supports the leaders of the organization. The management control system should be examined periodically and in detail by an outside agency, in order to ensure that it truly is serving your needs and those of the mission.

From time to time, leaders should delve into reports that staff agencies are submitting to higher headquarters. These reports often bring pressure upon subordinate associates, and there may be temptations to violate integrity. In other words, the documents that go to corporate headquarters may be sources of the breakdown of personal and institutional honesty and character. Some workers may be inclined to "fudge" numbers or manipulate results. Therefore, be aware that these documents are not foolproof. You may decide to perform occasional, but subtle, checks where possible.

Associates at lower levels within an organization can identify phony and/or weak leaders very rapidly and, therefore, are an excellent source of insight concerning subordinate leaders working for you. Someone who may look competent to you may look very different when viewed from below. Walt Ulmer, who has held many top executive positions and is the former president of the Center for Creative Leadership, feels that there should be subordinate input into personnel evaluations. Although this may be impracticable in a formal sense, there is a great deal of wisdom in Ulmer's point. Informal mechanisms can be helpful in ensuring that the top leader does not tolerate abysmal leadership on the part of one or more subordinate leaders. One useful approach is the use of 360-degree feedback mechanisms. These 360-degree systems are quite simple and effective. Instead of getting feedback only from your boss, you also get feedback from your peers and subordinates. In addition, there is a self-evaluation component of this multi-source feedback system.

Informal feedback through individuals who are not in the organizational hierarchy and who do not work directly for the top leader can also be effective. Retired associates who are keeping in close touch with friends who remain within the organization can be good sources of mature and objective feedback. The spouses' communication net can provide valuable insights, as well. Additionally, there almost always are "tuned-in" individuals who, although they do not occupy key positions within the hierarchical structure, can be helpful.

Gathering information through informal conversation among friends is an extremely effective feedback technique. A president of a multibillion-dollar corporation (and good friend) told Perry that the way he stays in touch with the various aspects of his organization is through lots of off-the-record phone calls from friends throughout his company and throughout his industry. This man possesses such extraordinary kindness and thoughtfulness that it is easy to see why he has such a vast network of friends and information. People like him and enjoy staying in contact with him and keeping him informed. His sincere charm and concern allow him to effectively tap into the undercurrents of his business.

Informal means of feedback should be used carefully. As a leader, you have a responsibility to support subordinate leaders and not to violate the established rules of hierarchy. On the other hand, not utilizing informal means of communication can be a mistake. Without good feedback from many sources, a leader is partially blind and, over time, can become isolated from the real problems and the real issues. Isolation diminishes the ability to anticipate problems, to receive innovative ideas, to maximize opportunities, and to serve as an enlightened and creative leader.

You should be particularly sensitive to feedback from members of groups who may feel, both collectively and individually, that they are "second-class citizens." If not given proper attention, these groups can become a source of poor morale and poor performance. There is

a dilemma here; while decentralization works to share power and
provide hands-on leadership, it also can lead to neglect of certain
groups, including maintenance staff and administrative and clerical
personnel. Make a special effort to give members of these groups
adequate time, support, and loving care.

15

REACHING OUT IN ALL DIRECTIONS

Building Bridges and Brain Trusts

■ ■ ■

A man should live with his superiors as he does with his fire;
not too near, lest he burn, nor too far off, lest he freeze.

—*Diogenes*

We must all hang together, or assuredly we shall all hang
separately.

—*Benjamin Franklin*

It's a given that well-rounded leaders have to work effectively within
their own organizations. In your role as a leader, either of an entire
company or of one division, you have to manage those who report to
you directly or indirectly, work cooperatively with your peers, and
nurture the relationship with your bosses. You are also ultimately
responsible for the organization's interaction with its clients, customers, stakeholders, and stockholders. Equally important, however, you
are an ambassador for your organization to outside institutions and
groups, even if they may not appear to have any direct connection
to or interest in your business.

Managing up, especially in large organizations, is almost an art
form. When you foster and maintain an atmosphere of mutual trust
that is based on loyalty and respect, everyone throughout the organization benefits. Of course, trust and respect come more easily when

the part of the organization for which you are responsible performs its duties, tasks, and missions in an outstanding way. But superior performance isn't a guarantee of cooperation and support from above. There are just too many factors that affect the dynamics between "higher headquarters" and you.

While you may expect that the upper echelons will serve the needs of the subordinate departments in achieving their goals, unfortunately this is not always the case. You must be wary when higher-ups ask unreasonable things of your people, put unwarranted pressures on them, or forget the true missions of both your sector and the overall organization—missions that *should* be perfectly aligned. If you are the leader of one sector of a large organization, it is your duty not only to ensure that you and your bosses see eye to eye on goals and how to achieve them, but also to act as a "heat shield" for your staff when the need arises. You can and should set standards for interactions that are appropriate within the organizational hierarchy or chain of command. It is a job that demands a diplomatic hand and mutual respect for everyone concerned.

Senior leaders want to know that their staff and the subordinate departments are working together. While you want to encourage your people to be innovative, independent, and responsible, when it comes to interdepartmental conflicts it is your job to handle problems in a tactful, thoughtful, and appropriate way. If there is a battle to be waged, gather the facts and engage in the conflict yourself—at the right time in the right way. Many large organizations have predetermined protocols for handling disagreements up and down the hierarchy and from one division to another. Know them and follow them. In other instances, common sense and common courtesy will direct your actions.

Whether you are a mid-level leader or the ultimate authority, how well you direct the flow of communication throughout the organization is of paramount importance. As we recognized earlier in this book, everyone has a boss. And everyone becomes a middle man between the higher-ups and the subordinate organizations. Reporting successes, problems, and solutions upward is equally as important as sharing with your people the higher headquarters' suggestions, concerns, and assessment of your group's performance.

Building partnerships with sibling organizations is a very important task and should be built upon respect and trust, if not affection. As the overall leader a multipart organization, you should have zero tolerance for "turf battles," destructive criticism, backbiting, and rumor mongering. It is your duty to clearly define the role and expectations of each division and to ensure that there is appropriate communication from the top down and from one part of the organization to another. This is true whether the perceived rivalry is between two production facilities in a manufacturing company, among branch offices of a bank, between the planners and the programmers, between the governor's office and the State Assembly, or between the Department of Defense and the Department of State.

As a leader of one division or another, you are responsible for your employees' actions but also, equally important, for negotiating with your upper management when disputes arise with a sibling division.

When you, your associate leaders, and your bosses work cooperatively and are open and honest in your communications and expectations, you avoid turning healthy competition into dysfunctional criticism, parochialism, and unproductive opposition.

Reaching Outward

Too many leaders bury themselves in day-to-day business activities and forget that success depends not only on the organization's financial performance but also in large part on the support of other groups, institutions, and organizations. Every organization is part of a larger community. From the town, area, or country in which you operate, to the professional associations with which your organization is aligned, to the social and other groups to which your employees belong, the involvement of you, your associates, and your organization will benefit you well beyond the public relations and goodwill your participation engenders. It behooves your organization not only to support those groups—from Little League to schools to charitable organizations—but also to encourage your employees to become engaged and, in the process, become ambassadors to the community at large. As the leader, you should be the model for your associates through the volunteer work to which you personally can commit.

And while you might be tempted to leave media relations to your PR and corporate communications department, establishing personal and trusted relationships on an ongoing basis with the media will set you up for a better experience in good times and times of crisis. Becoming a go-to person in your area of expertise is worth more advertising and paid promotion than you can imagine.

Brain Trusts

As you go about the business of building bridges—within and outside your organization—one natural outgrowth of this effort is the creation of a brain trust. You will inevitably gather about you an informal group of talented, principled advisors to whom you can turn when you face challenges or simply need a sounding board. Collectively or individually, the members of your brain trust will bring their own expertise and objective perspectives. The more you are open to their opinions—and vice versa—the more valuable this brain trust will be.

Of vital importance is the smaller and select group of advisors who function as an "ethical" brain trust. Those whom you choose to inhabit this inner circle will have strong records for taking ethical positions on important issues. Inevitably you are likely to run into situations that have important ethical components, and you will look to your most trusted advisors first as a sounding board and second to get advice on what is the best course of action.

16

MAKING THE TOUGH DECISIONS

Eight Useful Checks

■   ■   ■

In the long run men hit only what they aim at.
—*Henry David Thoreau*

After all is said and done, there is a lot more said than done.
—*Anonymous*

All true leaders are agents of change, as they create a strategic vision and take their organizations to higher levels of performance and excellence. The decision-making process is an important means by which leaders accomplish these goals. To make this element of your leadership most effective, make your decision-making process a systematic one.

From our experience in government and from observing a number of corporations at close hand, we have found that most senior leaders try to make too many decisions. Most decisions should be made at levels below the top; leaders should dedicate their precious time to the really key or sensitive decisions. It is a wise leader, indeed, who focuses most of his or her attention on the big decisions (a couple of dozen each year) and decisions that involve particularly sensitive issues (perhaps another dozen). Generally, if leaders attempt to make a much greater number of decisions, they fail in two areas. Either they are not fully informed on each issue or they are unable to ensure that the implementation process carries out the letter and spirit of the decisions. If a leader tries to do too much, he or she will, in the long run, accomplish too little.

Before you make a decision, ensure that complete coordination has taken place and that all important players, both inside and outside the organization, have had an opportunity to fully express their views. At any decision-making meeting, you should draw out the views of the quiet skeptics. This should bring to your attention the concerns of those who worry about the decision that you may be making. They can offer some useful cautionary comments about how your decision may backfire.

There are eight important checks to apply when preparing to make a final decision: the sanity check, the dignity check, the systems check, the media check, the safety check, the strategy check, the integrity check, and the implementation check. This eight-check rule has served us well not only as leaders, but as advisors to senior executives.

1. **The sanity check** is very simple, but quite important. Now that the coordination process is over and now that all of the delicate compromises have been made to get the key agencies and individuals to support the tentative decision, does the decision make sense? Have we created a Thoroughbred racehorse, a sturdy farm horse, or a camel with ten humps? The farm horse may be the best you can get, and you may have to be satisfied with that. But do not accept the camel. If a decision doesn't make sense, it is the obligation of the leader to reject it and to give guidance to his or her associates on how to proceed. It is not fair to your associates if a rejected decision paper is returned to them without some guidance from you on how to proceed.

2. **The dignity check** is also fundamental and uncomplicated. Will this decision enhance the reputation and dignity of this organization and its leaders, or will it undermine that reputa-

tion? If the latter is the case—if the decision "smells bad"—you should return the issue for further consideration. Furthermore, you should provide associates with some "top-down" guidance concerning your objections and offer suggestions on how to fix the problems.

3. **The systems check** requires a careful consideration of the various parts of the decision to ensure that there is internal consistency and coherency. Also does this decision fit within the goals of the organization? Even though individual parts of the decision may make sense when analyzed separately, all parts must fit together. A coherent decision has the best chance of being implemented in a way that will serve the interests of the leader and the organization. An airplane analogy illustrates this point well. The wings, fuselage, engines, cockpit, landing gear, and pilot must all fit nicely together or the airplane (the decision) will not fly—or if it does fly, it will not fly smoothly.

4. **The media check** involves a straightforward examination of how the decision will appear when it is reported in the print or electronic media. From our many years of work in the Pentagon, we have found this area of discussion to be most useful when it comes to stopping ourselves and our superiors from making foolish decisions. One effective technique is to try to frame a very critical headline and, at the appropriate time, to raise the issue this way: "I can see the headline and sub-headline in the paper next week—'National War College to Change Name to National Defense College: Still Studying War; Another Example of Defense Department Deception?' " The media receives a lot of criticism and much of it is deserved. However, if it wasn't for the media playing its role as watchdog and critic, the number of stupid decisions made in government, corporations, and elsewhere would increase significantly.

5. **The safety check** should take into consideration the physical and psychological safety of employees and customers alike. A corporation's products will be used by a large diversity of people. If a product emits low-level but dangerous radiation, if long-term use of the product leads to carpal tunnel syndrome, if a drug has side effects that can injure users, if a food product contains an excessively high level of bacteria, if your drivers are forced to work fourteen hour days in order to move your product to market, or if the ear protectors on your production line workers are not the best available, you as a leader must be aware, get involved, and take decisive action to fix the problem.

6. **The strategy check** is critical in determining how much a decision will help or hurt the future of the organization. When organizations have comprehensive long-range strategic plans, these plans were designed to facilitate major decisions. Generally, decisions need to be made that are consistent with the established priorities documented in the approved plan. If a decision is going to stray from the long-range plan, it needs to be very clear for all to see the rationale for such a decision. Decisions often make good tactical sense but fail the strategy check. In the early 1980s, IBM made a conscious decision to attack its own personal computer advocates because they were beginning to threaten the corporation's mainframe gurus. As a result, IBM lost its early edge in personal computer technology and allowed Hewlett-Packard, Dell, and Apple to gain a large market share. This is an example of the lack of a grand strategy, one that could incorporate both mainframe and personal computers. As another example, consider Japan's decision to bomb Pearl Harbor. If the Japanese leaders in 1941 had done an objective strategic analysis of the decision to launch that air

attack, they might have chosen another course of action. If they had questioned the key Japanese assumption that the United States would be willing to sue for peace after receiving a devastating sneak attack, strategic leaders might have said, "Now, wait just a minute." Japanese leaders should have checked themselves against American history. When Americans had perceived that they were attacked by foreigners—by the British in 1812, by the Mexicans at the Alamo, by the Spanish when the battleship *Maine* blew up, by the German U-boats on the high seas prior to American entry into World War I—the United States had reacted with strong military force. General Tojo and the other key Japanese leaders were brilliant tacticians, but poor strategic thinkers. They failed to conduct an objective strategy check.

7. **The integrity check** concerns the basic ethics issue. It concerns both the means and the ends of the decision, as well as the long-term reputation of the organization. In the interest of pursuing legitimate goals, have you selected unethical means to beat the competition, to fool the press, to outsmart the Congress, to beat your bureaucratic foe? Are the goals themselves ethical? The integrity check can be very useful as a deterrent to dishonorable, immoral behavior. If your associates know that you are going to conduct an ethical examination of every decision, they are more likely to find ethical means to reach ethical ends.

8. **The implementation check** forces you to ask a key question: Do we have the resources and support to carry out the decision I am about to make? If not, then the decision will be a bad one and should not be made. If you establish a pattern of making decisions that cannot be carried out, you will gain a reputation as an unreliable leader.

Leaders who limit themselves to making only a few decisions each month have the time to reflect on the important interrelationship between their strategic vision and their decisions. In contrast, leaders who race around putting out fires may get lots of psychic rewards from staying extremely busy, but the price they pay—reduced coherency and a weakened leadership vision—is likely to be quite high. As a leader, you should draw satisfaction not from the quantity of your decisions, but from their quality. Also, train yourself to get satisfaction not only out of the decision itself but also out of its full implementation.

17

LEADING DURING CRISES AND CHANGE

Keeping Cool and Flexible

■ ■ ■

> The Chinese use two brush strokes to write the word "crisis." One brush stroke stands for danger, the other for opportunity. In a crisis, be aware of the danger—but recognize the opportunity.
>
> —*Richard M. Nixon*

Mr. B is the principal of a very large racially and ethnically diverse high school in suburban Washington, DC. At a helpful workshop, he shared many of the difficulties he faced in recent years: suicides, attempted suicides, gang fights, drug incidents, sexual behavior between teachers and students, attempted rapes, etc. In response to these ongoing issues, he formed and trained a number of crisis response teams. He devised a system in which he has quick access to police and fire departments and nearby hospitals. He emphasized how important it was for principals and vice principals to be visible and approachable, so that they could be alerted ahead of time to conditions that students and faculty members found potentially threatening. Through quick action, such leaders can head off many crises and competently handle the ones that do develop.

In particular, one technique he used can be labeled "preemptive warning." He started spreading the word with tuned-in students that he was aware of some bad thing that was about to happen. He made it clear that he was willing and able to pass out severe punishment if the bad action was carried out. Moreover, he put the word out on what the punishment would be. If the act took place, this principal delivered the punishment as advertised.

This approach gives him credibility at a time of great tension and often stops the bad event from ever taking place. Mr. B uses the "language of the corridor" to get his message across. Without using profanity, he uses such terms as "If you do this, you are history," or "You do this and it's the highway." He is not afraid to demonstrate his strong emotional commitment to his school and to his standards. Since most of his students are devoted to his school and his program, his tough words have real impact, especially at times when emotions are running high. His presence in the halls and at all the major sporting events provides not only support for student activities, but also a deterrent to disruptive or violent behavior. This man is an effective leader who is more than a good crisis manager; he anticipates and heads off crises.

All of us live in a high-pressure world; it is not just the political leaders, police and fire department chiefs, hospital emergency room staff, or military leaders who have to deal with crisis situations. Principals, heads of nonprofits, and business leaders of all stripes must be prepared for a wide range of issues—from the poisoning of medications to toxic gas leaks to airplane crashes, and from hostile corporate takeover attempts to stock market crashes. A crisis for a small business owner may not seem so dramatic, but it can have a devastating impact on the business.

A crisis situation calls upon skills and leadership techniques that may not be exercised during a normal workday, and you may have to make decisions and take action when you're short on facts, when emotions are running high, or when the "fog of war" leads to much confusion.

Six major aspects of crisis leadership are preparation, decisiveness, flexibility, innovation, simplicity, and empowerment. One of your most important initial steps is getting the right people engaged. You need your best advisors and most knowledgeable people around you to help make the best decisions for the right reasons. You must be open to suggestions on how to solve crises, and be willing to allow emergent leaders to assist. A hallmark of crisis leadership is keeping things simple. Ask associates to do things that they are already trained to do. Try to avoid asking them to do new things with which they are unfamiliar.

In many acute crises, such as natural disasters, fires, industrial explosions, and combat firefights, leaders may not have the communications on hand to be able to handle the situation. Additionally, they may be isolated from the crisis (for example, taken hostage), be injured, have had a heart attack, or be incapacitated for other reasons. In anticipation of crises, you should identify and train other leaders who can grab the ball quickly and handle the problems.

As a crisis manager, you must be technically competent and must understand the people, the organization, the mission, the goals, and the priorities. You cannot operate with superficial knowledge of what the organization is about and what its capabilities are. In a crisis situation, it is of utmost importance to remain calm and dispassionate. You must keep an eye on individual performances, while holding the mission as the first priority. Although emotionally involved in the issues, you must try to stand back from the situation to make choices, which will ensure that the best possible solutions are achieved. In an extreme situation, this may mean sacrificing your or another's career, health, or life for the greater good of the largest number of people, or the greater good of the mission. Such situations often occur in combat.

One of our favorite combat stories took place in 1968 during the Vietnam War. Jack Jacobs, a twenty-two-year-old Army first lieutenant was serving as an advisor to a South Vietnamese Army battalion.

Jacobs was well trained, had lots of recent combat experience, and spoke Vietnamese, so he was well prepared for the next combat episode. His battalion was ambushed by a large enemy unit. In the first minute of the battle, a rocket exploded right in front of Jack, killing two of his fellow soldiers and shearing off part of Jack's head. Many of the bones in his face were broken and he could not see out of one eye. Yet, in the next five hours, Jacobs pulled many of his wounded buddies off an active battlefield. Each was dragged to an aid station where medical assistance could be received. Jacobs recounted what his thoughts were when he realized that many soldiers were badly wounded and needed assistance. A paraphrase of the words of Hebrew scholar Hillel flashed through Jack's mind: "If not me, who? If not now, when?"

Jacobs quickly realized that since all of his buddies were either wounded or dead, he had to take action. With the enemy methodically moving onto the battlefield and shooting his wounded buddies, he could not wait for a rescue team to help him. He felt he had to act and he had to do it right away. In the next five hours he saved the lives of thirteen wounded friendly soldiers. He received the Medal of Honor for his sustained period of extraordinary heroism. Combat and crisis leadership requires this kind of commitment to the welfare of people who may be in grave danger and may be receiving little or no help.

The parallel between combat leadership and crisis leadership is close, although lives are not always endangered in the latter. There are the same tensions, the same need for flexibility and innovation, and the same demand to keep things basic and simple. The motivational leadership required in combat often is needed during noncombat crises as well, to ensure that individuals work in close harmony. In combat, soldiers believe that they have a real chance to succeed. They trust and respect their leaders, have feelings of individual invulnerability, and believe it will be the enemy who will lose. During any type of crisis, those involved need to have the same sense of confidence. This stems from the leader, who needs to operate in a well-trained yet pragmatic way. You must not be tied inflexibly to the procedures, doctrines, or policies of the past, for they may not apply to the fast-moving conditions of the present.

A crisis often provides a very severe test of the horizontal and vertical cohesion of an organization. Organizations that are well led, where peer groups work well together (horizontal cohesion), and where warm relationships have been established between intermediate-level supervisors and their subordinates (vertical cohesion) often do well in a crisis.

In fact, these organizations can be strengthened by a crisis, because many people learn from the crisis and take pride that they have performed well during the stressful experience. For example, the Tylenol poisoning crisis actually made Johnson & Johnson a stronger corporation. The company performed quickly and decisively by pulling a huge amount of Tylenol off the shelves. The leaders remained calm and collected and refused to overreact to criticism. Johnson & Johnson's public image was enhanced as it developed better anti-tampering devices for its drugs.

A part of the preparation process in crisis management is the creation and training of an "opportunity team." This team should not be directly involved in the moment-by-moment management of the crisis. This team should be aware enough of the circumstances that they can sit back, analyze opportunities, and suggest actions. Because leaders are so busy managing the crisis, they often have no time to generate ideas concerning the accomplishment of things that could not be done under ordinary circumstances. A small, diverse group of innovators, perhaps the corporate long-range planning group, can provide the "Why don't we try this?" or "Have you thought of this option?" input. Thus, the organization can turn a crisis, which is both a challenge and a unique event, into an opportunity.

President John F. Kennedy's response to the Berlin crisis of 1961 (the infamous Berlin Wall was being built to keep East Germans from escaping to freedom) serves as an excellent example of a leader taking advantage of a crisis. Kennedy used that crisis as an opportunity to build up conventional military forces, to call reserves onto active duty, and to deploy units to Europe for deterrent value. He had an "opportunity plan" and he carried it out.

Franklin Roosevelt also took advantage of various world crises in the late 1930s and early 1940s to help prepare the United States for war. His initiation of a peacetime draft, lend-lease, and the "destroyer deal" are three examples. The first initiative helped prepare the nation for wartime needs by giving military training to over a million American troops. The last two initiatives helped the British at a time when they were desperately in need of military equipment to deal with the German threat. In helping the British, the United States was able to build up a defense industry even before we entered the war in December, 1941.

We all can learn from the lessons of major historical crises. In the immediate aftermath of the terrorist attacks against the United States on September 11, 2001, Perry provided commentary for three national new organizations: CBS Radio News, National Public Radio, and Prime Time America. He reminded these radio audiences that the lessons of Pearl Harbor and its aftermath could be applied to the massive crisis of 2001. After the Pearl Harbor attack, America, in close coordination with its allies, developed a grand strategy that consisted of identifying and targeting each enemy's "center of gravity," establishing a policy of unconditional surrender, and instituting a goal of creating, after the war, a working democracy in Japan, Germany, and Italy. In other words, by channeling our sense of outrage, the United States, with powerful support from its allies, was able to win the war and, even more importantly, win the peace. In 2001, America worked closely with many allies to create a counter-terrorism strategy that led to the deaths of many of the top Al Qaida

leaders, including Osama Bin Laden. Bin Laden was successful tactically, but he made a big strategic mistake—he helped unify the nations of the world in their pursuit of terrorists.

After a crisis is over, it is useful to conduct a "hot wash-up"—a wonderfully descriptive term used throughout the NATO alliance. The Army uses the term "after action review." Both target the same goal. The leader should bring together the key people involved in the crisis to analyze what happened. What went right? What went wrong or needs improvement? What lessons were learned and how do we decide what needs to be done to reduce the probability of repeating the same mistake? In addition, a report that includes an analysis of points or areas where future crises can be handled well should be completed.

A caution is in order when considering crisis leadership. Some leaders so thrive in a crisis environment that if a crisis does not exist, they will often create one themselves! This can be a way of gaining the attention of lethargic employees and getting them to work at a high level of commitment and energy. However, "created crises" can be quite disruptive and counterproductive. They can lead to cynicism and disgruntlement on the part of associates. Employees will roll their eyes up to the ceiling and say under their breath, "Here we go again."

If you notice that, as a leader, you spend your life bouncing from crisis to crisis, ask yourself, "How many of these crises are generated from within the organization itself?" Who knows—it may be your associates creating crises just to keep you busy or happy. Or you may be encouraging crises in order to spur on your associates. Both are bad tendencies and should be avoided.

Finally, as you counsel your associates in your annual one-on-one sessions, be sure to ask them to anticipate possible crises. When they see one coming, they should let you know quickly so you can work with them to head off the crisis. If that is not possible, you can, at a minimum, activate your crisis action team and your opportunity team with the goal of turning the upcoming crisis into an opportunity.

Crisis Leadership Checklist

The best leaders anticipate crises and prevent many of them from occurring. However, some crises cannot be anticipated and others cannot be prevented. Leading an organization successfully through a crisis is often very challenging. But it can also be an uplifting and strengthening experience for you and for your people. The following guidelines may help:

- ☐ Have a transition plan that shifts you from normal operations to crisis management.
- ☐ Quickly set up a work shift pattern—for example, establish twelve-hour shifts.
- ☐ Make decisions quickly but responsibly.
- ☐ Keep everything simple; don't give complex directions.
- ☐ Be flexible.
- ☐ Do not demand exactness or perfection.
- ☐ Expect things to get fouled up, and don't overreact when they do.
- ☐ Focus your attention on the next few days; try to avoid managing the crisis minute by minute.
- ☐ Form your "opportunity" team.
- ☐ Meet with this team at least once a day to get its ideas.
- ☐ Consider actions that could not be taken in a normal situation.
- ☐ Get adequate rest; over time, eighteen-hour days will diminish your performance and your objectivity.
- ☐ Get near the action.

☐ Set some priorities.

☐ Articulate the priorities to your associates.

☐ Follow the priorities.

☐ Develop a public affairs strategy.

☐ Keep in close contact with your lawyer and your public affairs expert.

☐ If there are adversaries:

   ☐ Outsmart them

   ☐ Operate within their decision cycles

☐ Thank people often.

☐ Keep training, if you can.

☐ Maintain high standards of ethics and dignity; sniff the air on a regular basis.

18

DEALING WITH THE DOWNSIDE

Failures, Rumors, and Criticism

■ ■ ■

Don't be discouraged by a failure. It can be a positive experience. Failure is, in a sense, the highway to success, inas-
much as every discovery of what is false leads us to seek
earnestly after what is true, and every fresh experience
points out some form of error, which we shall afterwards
carefully avoid.

—*John Keats*

A thick skin is a gift of God.

—*Konrad Adenauer*

When Perry was asked to speak to a thousand-member class at one
of the service academies, he assumed that he would be asked to speak
on leadership, or perhaps about his role as a military analyst for
various television networks. To Perry's surprise, the topic selected
was "Dealing with Failure." He may have been chosen to address
this subject because he had five major setbacks in his military career.
One of the most important qualities of a good leader is the capacity
to deal constructively with setbacks and failure. Having failed many
times both as a leader and as a subordinate, Perry understands that
failure is a marvelous learning and growing experience.

The following paragraphs outline failures that have occurred in
the lives of Perry and Jeff. They both have learned a great deal from

their personal setbacks. They have also learned to tolerate the failures of their associates and to identify with those experiences.

One of Perry's failures occurred when he was fired from a key position in the Pentagon. As an Air Force colonel, he was serving as a military assistant to the deputy secretary of defense Bill Clements. Perry's job was to attend meetings with the deputy secretary and to travel with him. He would take notes and ensure that Mr. Clements's decisions were carried out faithfully and promptly. Perry also had the responsibility to tell him privately when he thought Mr. Clements was getting bad advice or when Clements was about to make a decision that might backfire.

One day, Perry got a call from a friend who was responsible for all assignments for Air Force colonels. He told Perry that he had just received a new assignment and was being sent to Europe to be the chief of maintenance for a fighter wing in Germany. This was quite curious news since Perry had been working for the deputy secretary for only ten months. (The normal tour of duty was two years.) When Perry asked this personnel officer what the surprise assignment meant, he got a very frank answer: "Perry, you have been fired." The next morning, Perry asked the deputy secretary to explain what was happening. Mr. Clements told Perry that the Air Force wanted to get him back flying airplanes and that he was willing to let him go. The deputy secretary of defense, Bill Clements, made two major mistakes. He failed to tell Perry that he had fired him, and when asked directly by Perry, Clements lied. Perry learned a powerful lesson that he was able to apply later in his life: how not to fire someone.

It was the Perry's first major setback in life. It provided a wonderful lesson in humility. His family was very supportive. His wife, Connor, was happy to get him away from a frustrating job. Their two teenage children, McCoy and Serena, were delighted to learn that they would be living in Europe. Soon, Perry was focusing his full attention on checking out of the Pentagon and getting the family packed up for the flight across the Atlantic.

Some of his friends suggested that being fired was not such bad news. The senior leadership in the Air Force did not respect the deputy secretary of defense, and some of these top leaders felt that being fired was a plus and not a minus for Perry. Within two years of the date he was fired, Perry was given one of the best jobs in the Air Force, the command of the only F-15 fighter wing in Europe. But, alas, that assignment also would lead to failure. Hence, the next story . . .

Perry had four thousand people working for him at the time. The mission of the fighter wing was an important one: to defend Western Europe from air attack. At that time, the military threat was from the Soviet Union and other Warsaw Pact countries to the east. These countries had a much larger number of combat aircraft than did NATO, so Perry's job was especially challenging. As commander of the wing of eighty F-15s, Perry was responsible for conducting realistic training, for developing tactics for this wonderful new airplane, and for ensuring that the flying operation was conducted professionally and safely.

During a period of nine months, five brand-new F-15 fighter aircraft crashed. At that time, these airplanes cost about $20 million each. The problems centered around two issues: the F-100 engine and the aircraft's fuel system. Two weeks after the fifth airplane crashed, Perry learned, to his utter amazement, that the Air Force had promoted him from colonel to brigadier general. Normally, a wing commander is fired if he loses two airplanes; Perry had lost five.

About a month after his promotion was announced, Perry asked the commander of all U.S. Air Forces in Europe how he could possibly have been selected for promotion. The answer Perry got was fascinating. The general replied, "Because you handled failure well." The general told him that each wing commander throughout Europe was failing in one way or another. One had a major drug problem on his base, another had flunked a major NATO inspection, a third commander had a significant racial problem on his base, and yet another had a terrible ground-safety record. The general then explained that he learned more about the character and competence of leaders when they were dealing with failure than when they were succeeding.

Here is another example of Perry failing. In this case, Perry was not in a leadership position. He was the military analyst for CNN and had held that position for seven years. In 1998, CNN produced a special titled *The Valley of Death*. This special was scheduled as part of an hour-long show that was to be shown on a Sunday evening in June. *The Valley of Death* accused the U.S. Air Force of using lethal nerve gas during a secret combat operation in Laos in September 1970, during the Vietnam War. Five days before the special was to be shown, Perry learned about it. He tried to stop the special because he was almost sure that this had never happened. Sadly, Perry did not try hard enough, the special was shown, and CNN was in big trouble.

When Perry learned that gas was dropped but it was tear gas and not nerve gas, he had tried to get CNN to do a quick retraction, but he failed to adequately make his case. When it was clear that CNN was going to extend the story the following Sunday, Perry resigned in protest. He told the CEO of CNN that he "could not stand the ethics" and that he would never work for CNN again. The outcry against CNN from veterans of the Vietnam War was loud and sustained. Within ten days, the CEO called in an outside group to examine the issue. This group could not confirm any of the charges that CNN had made. A few weeks later, CNN did an on-camera retraction and fired the two producers of the special. However, the damage was done, and many viewers left CNN permanently. CNN's ratings went way down, and within a few months the network had given pink slips to more than four hundred employees. It was institutional failure of the first order, but Perry feels he should accept part of the blame: This failure might have been prevented if Perry had driven from Augusta to Atlanta, demanded that he look at the special before it was shown, and been much more aggressive in insisting that the special not be shown. Associates who observe an organization about to make a major mistake should be very aggressive in trying to stop a really bad decision from being implemented.

The leadership lessons of this debacle are clear. CNN had none of the safeguards that prevent ethical lapses. At the time this failure occurred, the network had no leadership training, no ethics training, and no ombudsman or inspector general. Although it produced a special on the military, it failed to contact its military expert during the nine months that the special was in production. In 1998, CNN was the number one ranking cable news channel in America. By the second decade of the twenty-first century, the network had fallen to number four.

Jeff had an experience early in his career that involved a highly decorated noncommissioned officer, Vietnam veteran, and technical genius. This man was also an alcoholic and chronically in debt. He was abusive with his soldiers and had virtually no effective leadership skills. Despite three months of focus-coaching to reform, this soldier was unable to turn his life around. He lost all respect from his subordinates. Ultimately he was administratively discharged from the Army—sadly, after fourteen years of service.

Jeff learned some important lessons from this experience. The entire organization was watching how Jeff and the leadership handled this situation. Compassion and counseling were followed by decisive action. This action was required to preserve good order and discipline in the unit. No effective team could have been built as long as this soldier remained a member of the organization.

As an Army captain, Jeff was unprepared for briefing a visiting high-level official on a critical issue confronting the organization. He completely missed identifying the background and existing knowledge base of the visiting dignitary. Soon after he started the briefing, Jeff was asked by this dignitary, "When are you going to tell me something I do not already know?" Jeff did not have an answer and was dismissed from the briefing room. It was a major embarrassment for him and for his organization.

What Jeff learned: he failed to properly prepare for the target audience. He also learned how relieved he felt when his senior leaders embraced him, underwrote his mistake, and told him he was going to be a better officer because of this experience. His leaders accepted blame for his failure . . . even though Jeff knew he really was at fault.

In a broader context, Jeff understands that he sometimes is guilty of excessive pride and ego. This damages his ability and willingness to listen. Too often he has been unwilling to consider alternative approaches or to accept criticism of his decisions. In some cases good ideas—potentially great ideas—never made it to the consideration table.

Since both Jeff and Perry have failed on many occasions, they tend to be quite tolerant when their associates and subordinates fail. History generally supports the viewpoint that good leaders turn failures into constructive experiences. Many people suffered setback after setback before they emerged as extraordinary leaders. Abraham Lincoln, Harry Truman, and Winston Churchill learned from their numerous failures and were strengthened and matured by these experiences. In the aftermath of every setback or failure, be sure to ask yourself two questions: "What have I learned from this failure?" and "How might I avoid making the same mistakes again?"

In addition to dealing with failure and intimidation, leaders must give considerable attention to other unpleasantries—handling the bad luck, the rumors, and the criticism. It is the responsibility of leaders to ensure that they maintain good communication and feedback loops relating to unfortunate events occurring within their organizations. These loops should be even better than those dealing with more normal and upbeat events. Leaders must not only actively seek out bad news, but also understand that there will be people at various levels trying to withhold such news from them. If they are not vigilant, the information they receive will be a mere portion of the total bad news within their organizations.

No matter how perceptive, aware, and "tuned in" you may be, illegal, unethical, or unfortunate activities will occur and will go unreported. Sexual harassment, racial slurs, petty theft, drug abuse, and alcoholism are the stuff of everyday life in some organizations. You must ensure that you have the procedures and the institutional support (auditors, health-care professionals, lawyers, crisis action teams, etc.) available to identify these problems and to solve them as expeditiously as possible.

You should have regular interaction with the lawyer or lawyers who work for you. These lawyers should be encouraged to be absolutely frank in their discussions. Decisions must be made on a regular basis as to whether an accused party needs to be counseled, given appropriate administrative punishment, or fired. Advice from lawyers is helpful concerning activities that someone is carrying out for the good of the organization, but that might be illegal or unethical. For example, fund-raising activities such as bingo games, raffles, or football pools may be prohibited by state or federal law or, in overseas areas, by local law or "status of forces" agreements.

The lawyer should be a very important advisor—an individual who has a high level of integrity, is energetic and "tuned in," and believes in maintaining an appropriate balance between the rights of individuals and their obligations to the organization. Listen carefully to your lawyer(s). Although you may want to overrule an attorney, this should be done only after careful analysis. An individual with substantial legal training and experience can contribute greatly to your thinking and decision-making.

Some leaders moan and groan whenever the subject of rumors, rumormongers, and the rumor mill comes up for discussion. Yet rumors can be very useful in large organizations and very helpful in a number of ways. If you stay tapped in to the rumor mill, you will learn a great deal. Many rumors are factual, or at least are based on some factual data. Others give you blazing flashes of insight into where problems may be within the organization. Some rumors are wrong, and some can be dangerous. But even these can serve a good purpose, for they may alert you to an area that deserves immediate attention. Often, you can stamp out the bad rumor quickly with decisions or facts (or both) before it does too much damage. There may be times when the ugliness—perceived or factual—goes public. This is likely to touch your emotional side and tempt you to engage. Resist the temptation to dive into a pigsty—for everyone will get muddy. Get the appropriate counsel, maintain the ethical high ground, be professional, do what is right.

Upcoming personnel actions often spark rumors that permeate an organization: X is about to be fired; Y is in line for that vacant vice president's job; Z will be the next big boss. Unfortunately, these rumors sometimes cause individuals a lot of unnecessary trauma, concern, and disappointment. Yet it is impossible to stop them from spreading. A leader can, however, reduce the number and the impact of personnel rumors by being decisive, realistic, and, most of all, honest. A leader who procrastinates on personnel actions or who allows a cumbersome and lengthy personnel selection and promotion system to develop, permits unnecessary time delays and encourages rumors.

Leaders sometimes forget that, through their indecision or procrastination, they can be directly responsible for heartbreak. This is especially true when a rumor circulates about someone's promotion and it does not materialize. In this regard, one approach that can be taken with staff members and subordinate leaders is as follows: "We all know that there are many important personnel activities coming up this summer. There is no way we can stop the rumors between now and the time that the big boss makes up his [her] mind. If you don't know anything and want to speculate, be my guest. However, if you are privy to inside information, please don't say anything to anybody. If the boss changes his [her] mind, some people may be terribly disappointed."

Those individuals who have reached high leadership positions without one or more major setbacks in their careers are often not well equipped to handle failure and heavy criticism. Therefore, when you are choosing individuals for leadership jobs, you may wish to look into their backgrounds to see if they have met failure and, if so, how well they handled it.

When an organization suffers a major setback, the leader should be quick to accept the blame. It is the leader's fault that the organization failed because of poor planning, poor leadership, poor organization, or the inability to anticipate potential problems. There is always a temptation to blame subordinates, fate, poor quality of equipment, lack of guidance from above, or over-tasking. The leader should avoid these temptations. To quote the great Alabama football coach the late Bear Bryant, "There are just three things I ever say. If anything goes bad, then I did it. If anything goes semi-good, then we did it. If anything goes really good, then you did it. That's all it takes to get people to win football games."

Fear of failure is one of the major causes of stress for leaders, but you should welcome an occasional setback. Failure often demonstrates that the organization is trying new approaches, setting ambitious goals, and being creative. As a leader, you should identify some of these setbacks as "heroic failures that taught us all" and some as those which, at a later time, may turn into grand successes. Such an approach will help everyone to bounce back from failure. By recognizing the value of failure and complimenting your people on the initiatives they've taken, you can encourage everyone to continue to reach beyond his or her grasp in order to accomplish great things. This is a technique that Bill Gates and Steve Ballmer used with extraordinary success at Microsoft. By encouraging their associates not to be afraid of failing, they liberated a powerfully creative workforce to think and act "outside the box."

The higher the post you occupy, the more strictly you will be judged. A leader is bound to be criticized, both fairly and unfairly, by associates within the organization, by bosses and staffs, by competitive organizations, and by the press. A leader who becomes thin-skinned when criticized, or who becomes defensive and somewhat paranoid, is doing a disservice to the organization. As a leader, it is important that you observe how well your associates accept criticism and how willing they are to accept blame for the failures of the organization. The defensive "blame someone else" individual is unlikely to succeed as a leader. By admitting a failure early on, leaders often take necessary corrective action and return the organization to a higher level of performance and morale.

19

HANDLING THE MEDIA

Building Important Partnerships

■ ■ ■

I fear three newspapers more than one hundred thousand bayonets.

—*Napoléon*

Meeting the press fairly and squarely is a challenge for many leaders. But if you are one of those who makes it a policy to avoid contact with the media, you may miss the chance to learn and grow from the crucible that an active free press provides. Even more important, the media offers an avenue through which you can get proper recognition for your organization and people.

Most mid- to large-size companies and organizations have strategic communications or public relations offices to work with the media and other outside interest groups on a regular basis. Effective offices have developed strategic communications plans that serve the interests of the organization. These offices monitor what the media has to say about the organization (as well as other topics of interest and concern to the organization), issue press releases, and set up press conferences. They generally take a proactive approach to engaging the public via the media. In working with management at all levels, they develop plans and policies to deal with a wide range of issues to ensure that there is a consistent message. Depending on the situation, the communications department may take the initiative to release information according to your timetable or wait until a request is received.

Depending on the size and visibility of your organization, media relations may be handled in any number of ways—by your public relations office, by designated spokespeople, or by you directly.

Be Prepared

Working in concert with your own communications professionals, you should establish ground rules for how your organization handles the media. While most mature organizations will already have set policies, you and your company's media relations department should reflect how you wish to see the company perceived. It is vital that you understand how you, as well as your organization, may be perceived by the press, since you will want to either enhance a positive reputation or overcome a negative one.

Regardless, one of the most important actions you can take early on in your leadership role is to develop a trusted relationship with the key media influencers in your community. This means identifying the credible sources and getting to know them—without any agenda other than learning about each other. These relationships will pay dividends when real events—good or bad—capture the media's attention.

To the fullest extent possible you should control every encounter with the media and establish the guidelines under which any interview will be conducted. You should set the agenda, and your answers to the interviewer's questions should announce that agenda loud and clear.

Will an interview be on or off the record? Will you have the opportunity to see the manuscript or the videotape before it is released? If not, why not? It generally is useful to speak informally with the reporter before you get into the actual interview, in order to find out whether that reporter has any major preconceptions or misconceptions. If so, you can try to correct or rectify these misconceptions before the interview begins. If you cannot set things straight, be particularly wary of what you say. When media representatives have already made up their minds, it is for you often a question of trying to "limit damage" as much as possible. If a member of the media is clearly biased, you have a responsibility to alert your bosses and the public affairs people at higher levels to let them know that a critical or misleading article or program soon may appear, despite your best efforts.

If a reporter is willing to show the draft of an article to you before it goes to press, you have a chance to correct errors or to expand on some important points. Many responsible journalists will allow you to help them if you have established an atmosphere of mutual trust and respect. Communicating directly and regularly with the media, giving them the opportunity to observe firsthand what your organization does, and offering them the chance to see some things that they would not normally see are some useful techniques to help establish a positive rapport between you and news professionals, as well as to break down the natural barriers that often exist.

Frequently, when media representatives interview a leader, they don't ask the best questions. If you feel comfortable with those who are asking the questions, you often can steer them in the right direction. For example, if the interviewer asks a question that is not particularly relevant, you can provide an answer and then say, "That was a good question, but I think there is a better question along the following lines." Then you ask the question and answer it yourself. This will educate the media representative, and he or she very well may pick up on your points. Thus, the interview will become more productive. Members of the media often spread themselves so thin across so many issues that they really don't know what questions to ask. You can help them ask the best questions. This technique puts you in charge of the interview and helps to tell the story you want to tell.

Leaders should consider the audience and empathize with their concerns about the issues at hand. Be straightforward in your answers to questions and avoid jargon and technical language that may not be understood. "I don't know" can be the best answer because it is an honest answer. The audience will respect you for admitting that you are not an expert on all matters. Stating that you do not know the answer to a question allows you to get to the next question quickly. And if you "wing it" and guess, the follow-up questions on the same subject will often destroy your credibility.

Members of the media are always looking for a "news hook": something interesting on which to hang the story. A leader can help provide such hooks if he or she is sensitive to the needs of the press and reaches out to associates to get ideas on how to bring newsworthy issues to the attention of reporters. The flip side of this point is also true. A leader can use upcoming news conferences as a means to encourage associates to come up with courses of action that will benefit the organization. For instance, President Kennedy used his biweekly press conference to accelerate the decision-making process, to keep informed on current issues, and to make policy decisions.

Some large organizations have a media-training program for leaders that gives them a chance to face various media challenges in a well-simulated environment. During this training, the following practice sessions are videotaped: a one-on-one interview, a general news conference, a confrontational news conference, a remote interview, and a speech followed by a question-and-answer format. The leader is then critiqued on style, body language, sense of humor, speaking voice, etc. To conduct this training many organizations hire consultants who specialize in media relations. You should take this training yourself and encourage those who are destined to move up the leadership ladder to sign up also. It is a half a day well spent.

Although some have argued that America has developed into a massive adversary culture in which the media's disparagement of all our institutions has become the norm, mature leaders can find ways to work positively with representatives of the news profession. Leaders of large organizations cannot hide from the media. These executives should meet often with their public affairs officers and seek their guidance, criticism, and support.

Finally and perhaps most importantly, leaders must ask themselves honestly how firmly committed they are to freedom of the press and a robust First Amendment. The leader who tends to be secretive, who feels the media is not a responsible element in society, or who is uncomfortable when in contact with members of the press is likely to be treated unfairly by the media, with sometimes critical or biased articles. Leaders of organizations in all areas of society must understand that they will have some media attention and must conduct their personal and professional lives with that fact in mind.

Press Conference and Media Interview Checklist

With the explosive growth of the media in recent years, it is not just heads of state, foreign dignitaries, senators, governors, mayors, generals, and CEOs of major corporations that meet regularly with reporters and journalists. Leaders at many levels must be prepared to interact, often on short notice, with the members of the media. This checklist can be a useful guide as you prepare for your next interview or press conference:

☐ Am I the right person to face the press? If not, who would be the most appropriate and credible spokesperson?

☐ What is the rationale for the interview or press conference? What agenda do I wish to pursue?

☐ Who will be the media representatives? What are their backgrounds, biases, and reputations for fairness?

☐ What issues are particularly sensitive for me, my boss, or my organization? What tough questions can I expect on the issues or about me? Am I prepared to answer these questions? If not, how can I appropriately deflect them?

☐ Do I have a written statement to give or to read to the media? Have I studied it closely to be sure that it conforms to policy and that I am comfortable with it?

☐ Will the interview be on or off the record?

☐ When would a press conference be in order? What form will it take? How long will it last? Will there be an open question-and-answer session? How will the press conference be terminated?

☐ Will the interview or press conference be televised? Will it be live or on tape?

☐ Will I get to see an advance copy of the script or an edited tape?

☐ What mistakes have been made by spokespersons in my organization that I wish to correct?

☐ If I expect a hostile session, how can I reduce the hostility?

☐ What are the three top messages I want to get across to the media regardless of what the media wants from me?

20

LEADING NONPROFITS

The Unique Challenges and Opportunities

■ ■ ■

The only ones among you who will be really happy are those who will have sought and found how to serve.

—*Helen Keller*

De Tocqueville, the French philosopher who toured America almost two hundred years ago, identified a trait throughout American towns and villages that he found extremely important. This trait was the strong tendency of Americans to form many associations at the local level that work for the common good. He felt that this admirable trait was very helpful in making democracy work in what was then a new republic. Happily this aspect of the American culture and character is still very much in evidence today.

Nowhere do the lessons of reaching out beyond your organization benefit an organization more than in the nonprofit sector. Leading nonprofit organizations presents challenges that are in many ways different from those within corporations, government institutions, and the military. From sources of funding to an often largely volunteer workforce, nonprofits may benefit from your corporate leadership experience but require that you bring a host of other talents into play.

With the exception of the very large nonprofits (such as large foundations and megachurches), most people who work in the nonprofits (museums, churches, temples, civic clubs, foundations, veterans groups, the Boy Scouts, the Girl Scouts, the Salvation Army, Goodwill Industries, Boys and Girls Clubs, soup kitchens, arts groups, etc.) are volunteers.

In many cases these volunteers work on a part-time basis and receive no compensation. They are often asked to dig into their pockets to provide financial support to the institutions that they have volunteered to serve. One of the great and abiding strengths of the American culture is the willingness of a high proportion of its citizenry to do their civic duty and donate their time, talents, and treasure to serve good causes.

Let's assume that you are the president of the board or a committee chairman of one of these nonprofits. The civic-minded people with whom you are working are admirable in so many ways. You need to thank them constantly. Also you should remind yourself often that your levers of power and authority over them are quite limited. After all, they are volunteers who receive no pay.

You cannot threaten to reduce their compensation if they are not performing well. You cannot demand that they put in extra hours to accomplish a task. If they miss meetings, arrive late to meetings, or fail to carry out their commitments, your ability to discipline them is severely constrained. Hence your skills at motivation and negotiation become very important.

One way to reduce difficulties with volunteers is to recruit board and committee members very carefully, seeking out those who are self-starters, energetic, and well connected throughout the community. One way to help reinforce the need for action-oriented people is to provide those great candidates a written invitation to become a member of the board or committee, describing in sufficient detail the obligations that come with the position. Some organizations even go a step further, by asking the invitee to sign a confirmation of intent or pledge to contribute some specific resource (like time or

$$) for the cause. As you strengthen the board or the committee that you chair, something quite amazing takes place—a virtuous circle is created. It becomes easier and easier to recruit new members. Board and committee candidates will want to join a team that consists of outstanding citizens who have the reputation for getting things done and done well. In short, the stronger the board, the even stronger it becomes.

Board members who turn out to be lazy, incompetent, or disruptive can and should be eased off the board. Your fellow board members will be happy to see these nonperformers leave, but they will want you to make their departure a dignified one. At a minimum they should be given letters of appreciation as they depart the board.

One common characteristic of many boards and committees that is found in many nonprofits is the unwillingness to make tough decisions. This is especially the case when there are votes on both sides of an issue. Hence, boards and committees should be made up of an odd number of members. Hence, a committee of nine is better than a committee of eight or a committee of ten. Having an odd number of members ensures that when it is time to vote, there are no ties. The best model is perhaps the Supreme Court, which has nine justices.

Fund-raising is almost always a key aspect of the work within the nonprofit sector. If you are in a leadership position, there is no way for you to avoid playing a role in gaining financial support. The best approach for you as a leader is a proactive one. First, make a financial commitment yourself; second, recruit a fund-raising committee of especially generous, well-connected, and well-respected individuals (people who have a natural talent for sales and marketing are the best). Third, set a funding goal for the campaign. Fourth, set a deadline for the completion of the campaign. Fifth, get some "lead donors" to make major commitments prior to the official opening of the campaign. Sixth, quickly thank each person or group who makes a contribution. Seventh, when the goal is reached, issue a press release and hold a celebration. Eighth, send a thank-you note (hand-written notes are best) to everyone who helped raise the needed funds.

Your role as leader of the fund-raising effort is to fire up these people with enthusiasm for the mission of the organization. To cite a specific example, recently the Augusta Museum of History decided to initiate a new symposium to honor Augusta's greatest hero, Lieu-tenant Colonel Jimmie Dyess, U.S. Marine Corps Reserve. Dyess is the only person to have received America's two highest awards for heroism, the Medal of Honor and the Carnegie Medal. The fund-raising goal was $50,000. Early in the campaign, lead donors were found. One gave $10,000 and four others gave $5,000. Hence when the formal campaign began the museum could state that it had already passed the halfway mark.

The next step that was taken was to reach out for contributions of $1,000. A number of "goodies" were offered to those who would commit at that level: (1) an invitation to a private reception for the honorees at the symposium; (2) a copy of the biography and the DVD on Jimmie Dyess; (3) a membership in the museum and a number of free passes to the museum; (4) a Medal of Honor history book— autographed by a Medal of Honor recipient; (5) reserved seating at the symposium.

The Jimmie Dyess Symposium has become a permanent part of the Augusta cultural experience. It is held the second Thursday in January each year. It also has become the most successful fund-raising effort of the Augusta Museum of History—an award-winning museum that struggled financially during the second decade of the 21st century.

Fund-Raising Checklist

Every nonprofit needs money to fulfill its mission. Volunteers may make up the bulk of the workforce, but, unless the nonprofit you are running is fully funded by some other agency or angel, its ability to function will depend on raising funds. The following checklist is a bare-bones outline of what an effective fundraising campaign entails. For more detailed information, consult the books listed below or other trustworthy sources online, such as the Association for Fundraising Professionals.

☐ Review and understand the mission of the organization.

☐ Set challenging fund-raising goals and determine specifically what the money will fund.

☐ Make an early and generous contribution yourself.

☐ Require every board member to make a specific "give or get" commitment.

☐ Recruit board members who have demonstrated a strong commitment to good causes. The more prominent the board, the easier it is to recruit new outstanding members and, in turn, to solicit contributions from major donors.

☐ Research prospective donors—corporations, funds, foundations, etc.—to determine how their missions match yours.

☐ Keep two lists: those who have been generous in the past and those who have not.

☐ Throw your net out very widely and include all parts of your community.

☐ Set deadlines to help focus on priorities.

☐ Never prod someone soon after he or she has just contributed.

☐ State the case: ask for the gift; aim high!; always ask big—if you hope to get $10,000, ask for $100,000.

☐ Be bold but not brash—always remember that you may need to go back and ask again.

☐ Don't get discouraged; lots of gifts take more than one request.

☐ Don't waste time going after individuals, businesses, or foundations that do not show any interest.

☐ Remind yourself often that your great cause may not be high on someone else's priority list.

☐ Remind yourself often that donors are being asked to support worthy causes all the time; understanding donor fatigue is important.

☐ Be careful of templates; techniques that work in one setting may not work in another.

☐ Publicize your projects widely; many public relations and advertising companies will do pro bono work.

☐ Remain very visible throughout the community.

☐ Staff must be prepared and willing to participate in all fundraising planning and activities.

☐ Closely monitor budgets—err on the lean side.

RESOURCES

For those interested in gaining greater knowledge and insights into leadership within a nonprofit, the following books (and website) are recommended. Be sure to get the latest edition of each.

How to Form a Nonprofit Corporation, 10th Edition, by Anthony Mancuso
Effective Fundraising for Nonprofits: Real-World Strategies That Work, 3rd Edition, by Ilona Bray
Mega Gifts: Who Gives Them, Who Gets Them, 2nd Edition, by Jerold Panas
The Association of Fund Raising Professionals: www.afpnet.org

PART IV

Bringing It All Together

21

FINAL THOUGHTS

Thirty Fundamentals of Leadership

■ ■ ■

A leader is a man who has the ability to get other people to
do what they don't want to do, and like it.

—*Harry S. Truman*

Leadership and learning are indispensable to each other.

—*John F. Kennedy*

This book has been designed to give you practical ideas on how to
develop yourself as a leader, how to improve your skills in leading
others, and how to lead organizations. Although this book provides
a number of checklists, it is important to emphasize that complete
reliance on "checklist" or "cookbook" leadership can be a mistake.
You should accept the ideas, insights, and checklists that are provided
with a certain amount of skepticism. Much that happens in any
organization is unique; however, the lessons of others may be helpful
as you face current challenges. What follows is a comprehensive
summary of the thirty key fundamentals that form the basis of our
approach to leadership.

1. Trusting

Leaders of large organizations must be able to trust subordinate
leaders and other associates. The motto should be: trust people and
make that trust predictable. This is a difficult task for those who

want to direct every aspect of their organizations. Such leaders cannot find their way clear to trust people, and as a result, they do not nurture sub leaders or give them the opportunity to exercise their creative talents. Being a truly effective leader requires a great deal of trust in associates, balanced with a willingness to remove people who cannot be trusted—a facet of leadership that necessitates tough decision-making. Without trust and other elements of mutual respect among leaders and their associates, an organization often will suffer a combination of low performance and poor morale. Avoid sending out "I don't trust you" messages such as "I never want to be surprised" or "When I am on the road, I'll check in every morning." In the words of Frank Crane, "You may be deceived if you trust too much, but you will live in torment if you do not trust enough."

2. Teaching

Teaching and leading go hand-in-glove. Leaders must be willing to teach skills, to share insights and experiences, and to work very closely with people to help them mature and become more creative. In order to be good teachers, leaders must be well-organized individuals, good communicators, and goal-setters. Push your organization up the "wisdom pyramid," take it from data to information to knowledge to wisdom. By teaching, leaders can inspire, motivate, and influence associates at all levels.

3. Communicating Creatively

Effective leaders master the written and spoken word, to create good communication that is meaningful, understandable, and actionable—both up and down the organization. Whether it's issuing directives, stating missions, or giving compliments, creative communication will inform, instruct, and inspire—and is fundamental to effective leadership.

4. Work Constantly

I never learned anything wh.

—Larry n.

Every day do some networking. Work constantly to expand your brain trust, to seek out creative and imaginative people, and to find innovative ideas. Exercise your curiosity and the curiosity of everyone you are in contact with. Constantly ask questions. Here are some examples: What is the most exciting idea you have uncovered recently? Who is the most creative person you know? What ideas has he or she shared with you lately? What is the best book you have read recently? What did you learn from that book? What are your favorite websites? Tell me something I don't know.

5. Avoiding the Role of Chief Problem Solver

Never tell people how to do things. Tell them what needs doing and they will surprise you with their ingenuity.
 —General George Patton

Leaders should facilitate problem-solving but should let associates solve most problems. The psychic reward—the sense of achievement—that someone gets from actually solving a problem is invaluable. It builds self-esteem and enhances one's ability to do even better in future situations. Even though leaders often can solve the problems more quickly than others, it is poor practice to be the problem solver. There are, of course, occasional exceptions. When the organization is in serious trouble or when associates are unable to formulate a workable solution, the leader may need to step in and select the best course of action. This works fine if the leader has better expertise, understanding, or contacts than his or her associates. However, organizations thrive best if the leader is the *problem solver of last resort.*

6. Building Stamina

The demands of leadership are very heavy. No matter how well executives may plan their daily, weekly, and monthly schedules, there will be times when the pressures and demands will be onerous. Even though leaders may be very tired, they must be able to reach within themselves to find the reservoir of energy and creativity to handle crisis situations and other tough decisions. Both a mental and a physical fitness program are essential for leaders who wish to be prepared for these difficult periods. Fundamentally, if leaders cannot take care of themselves, how can they create climates that provide care for others?

7. Managing and Using Time Effectively

One of the great faults of American leaders is their general failure to discipline their schedules, emails, in-boxes, telephones, travel commitments, and meetings. American executives are often caught up in "activity traps" that fill up their days, keep them very busy, and allow little time for thoughtful reflection and strategic thinking. Staying busy and working very long hours are not good measurements of leadership effectiveness. Leaders should control their schedules.

8. Maintaining Technical Competence

Executives must understand their businesses so that as they carry out day-to-day activities, they know what they are doing. Leaders not only must understand the major elements of the organizations that they head, but must also keep up with the changes. Otherwise, they cannot grasp exactly what their daily activities produce. Furthermore, if leaders have a high level of technical competence, then they should be able to trust their intuition. This combination of competence and intuition can be extremely powerful. They should ask themselves if they are satisfied with their own decisions, if their associates' decisions are acceptable, or if something seems wrong. To quote Ralph Waldo Emerson, "The essence of genius is spontaneity and instinct. Trust thyself." Part of intuition is having "antennae" out, keeping a hand on the pulse of the organization and being "street-smart" and "in touch." In other words, effective leaders should take a second look when things seem suspicious or smell bad.

9. Dealing with Incompetence

Leaders must be willing to set standards, to abide by those standards unwaveringly, and to require their associates to live by those standards. They are responsible for ensuring that missions are accomplished. Inhibitors to this task, such as the continued presence of ineffective associates, drain the organization and its leaders of the time, energy, and attention needed to accomplish goals. In such circumstances, leaders have a responsibility to remove those who stand in the way of success. Almost everyone within a given organization knows who is competent and who is not. The leader's actions (or nonactions) in dealing with incompetent people are seen by all. By allowing incompetent associates to stay in positions of responsibility, leaders are not serving themselves, the institutions, and, in many cases, the incompetent employees well. When it is necessary to remove people from key positions, leaders should meet personally with those individuals. Removals should be done with grace and style, but also with firmness. To quote an executive from a large hospital in Augusta, "Incompetence is the cancer that is destroying my hospital."

10. Taking Care of People

Leaders should recognize not just the top performers, but also the many others who are competently doing their jobs with good attitudes and a strong commitment to institutional goals. Making continuous efforts to thank people—during the morning, at noontime, and before leaving in the evening—is an important part of taking care of them. Acts of gratitude contribute to their psychological health. Furthermore, leaders should mentor outstanding associates while avoiding the pitfalls of cronyism.

11. Providing Vision

Leaders who are not planners are simply caretakers, gatekeepers, and time-servers. Though they may run efficient and effective organizations, leaders do not serve the long-term interests of their institutions unless they plan, set goals, polish their skills of anticipation, and provide vision and strategic leadership. Good planning, goal-setting, and priority-setting can accomplish these things and create a marvelous legacy. Leaders who are not visionaries should maintain frequent contact with people who have a talent for long-range planning, farsighted thinking, and innovation. By allowing visionaries to be heard, leaders can validate the process of creative, "out-of-the-box" thinking. The most effective leaders are agents for change, and one of the best ways to ensure change is through good strategic planning.

12. Controlling Ambitions and Egos

Often leaders need to suppress their strong personal ambitions. They should focus on mission accomplishment at the highest standards of excellence, integrity, and performance. Selfless leaders gain the respect of associates and the support of superiors. They are willing to say, "I was wrong," "I made a mistake," "I take full responsibility for the failure," and "I am willing to accept the full

consequences of that failure." If leaders are too ambitious for themselves, they may drive the organization in unfortunate directions.
In fact, they often become part of the problem rather than part of
the solution.

13. Planning and Conducting Meetings

Leaders spend much of their time in meetings. They should establish the ground rules and be actively involved in the meetings to
make sure that they stay on track. Scheduled meetings should have
announced start and stop times so that everyone can plan the rest
of the day; for instance, "The 11 a.m. sales meeting will end at noon."
As the meeting progresses, every attendee should be given ample
opportunity to express his or her views and disagreements. It is
important to know how to wrap up meetings, to draw conclusions,
to set up the time and agenda for the next meeting, and to direct
individuals to carry out certain tasks that have resulted from decisions made. An effective way to conclude a meeting is for the leader
to repeat what he or she has heard and to ask if any major points
have been missed (or misunderstood). Also, leaders must discontinue
regular (weekly, monthly, or quarterly) meetings that are not serving
an important purpose. American leaders must fight the cultural
tendency to hold long, undisciplined meetings that yield little useful
output.

14. Motivating

Leaders must not only know how to motivate in general, but they
should also teach their subordinate leaders so that they, in turn, will
develop strong motivational skills. Leaders of larger organizations
cannot reach all of their people on a regular basis, so they must count
on subordinate leaders to provide much of the motivation. Commitment to mission, love of the job and the people, dedication to high
standards, having fun, frequent reinforcement of the organization's

plans and goals, strong incentive and reward programs, and lots of compliments for hard work and high performance are all parts of the vital motivation factor.

15. Being Visible and Approachable

The four-hour rule is a useful guide: Leaders should spend no more than four hours a day in their offices. During the rest of the time, they should be out with their people, conducting meetings and visiting subordinates in their work areas. Good leaders pat people on the back, make brief and upbeat speeches, hand out awards, and travel widely throughout their establishment or business. In addition, effective leaders make contact with sister organizations, as well as with organizations at higher levels, so they can ensure that important relationships are enhanced and that problem areas are identified as early as possible.

When they are having meetings or discussions in their offices, leaders should never sit behind their desks. Instead, they should go to a couch or a sofa, thus avoiding an imposing position that is intimidating to associates. Visitors are more comfortable, and therefore more candid, when leaders sit in the more sociable areas of their offices. The visitors should feel that nothing is more important than the subject that they have come to discuss.

16. Using Humor Well

Most of the time, leaders should laugh at themselves rather than at others. They should tell jokes on themselves and share embarrassing stories about their own mistakes. This lets others know that they are human, that they err, and that they are willing to admit fouling things up. Good leaders demonstrate that life is not so serious that you can't kick back occasionally and be amused by what's happening. Humor can be a great reliever of tension; a story or an appropriate joke at times of crisis or difficulty can be very therapeutic. Use humor to amuse, not abuse. Humor that is delivered with an acid tongue and aimed at associates can be very counterproductive. Avoid off-color humor since it diminishes the dignity of leaders and organizations. In addition, leaders should not treat *everything* as a subject for humor. Nonstop comedians are unlikely to get the respect they need to be effective leaders and executives.

17. Being Decisive

Leaders must be decisive but not jump as soon as the first individual makes a recommendation for a decision. They should listen to all sides before deciding. In fact, on occasion, it is good practice for a leader to postpone an important decision for a day or two, or even a week or two, while collecting additional information. Leaders should always look for contrasting views and, if at all possible, sleep on important issues. They should talk to their assistants, deputies, spouses, or other people who can be trusted to forgo personal or parochial interests. In addition, leaders also should talk to people who disagree with the tentative decisions, to find out what their opposing views might be. However, postponing decisions for many weeks or months is rarely the answer. A nondecision is itself a decision. Risk-taking is frequently an essential and healthy aspect of decision-making.

Also, leaders must understand how to implement decisions. Decisions are of little use if they are not acted upon using well-thought-out strategies. Furthermore, there must be follow-up systems to ensure that decisions are not only carried out, but carried out faithfully in both substance and spirit.

18. Observing Themselves

Each person is really five people: you are who you are; you are who you think you are; you are who your subordinate associates think you are; you are who your peers think you are; and you are who your boss thinks you are. Leaders who work hard to get feedback from many sources are more likely to understand and control their various selves and, hence, be better leaders. They should be able to look at themselves objectively and analyze where they have made mistakes, where they have turned people off, and where they have headed down the wrong path. Leaders must be able to look in the mirror and determine what they did right today, what they did wrong today, to which decisions they need to return, and how approachable they were. They should ask themselves if they have been too narrow or too rigid. Trusted confidants can be very helpful in this continuous process of introspection.

19. Practicing Reliability

A leader should be careful about what commitments are made. Once a commitment is firm, nothing short of major health problems or a very serious crisis should alter it. Leaders must possess reliability in order to provide stability and strength to their organizations. Important aspects of reliability are persistence and consistency. Leaders should be reasonably flexible, but steadfastness and coherence are important elements of all organizations and deserve the support of leaders at all levels.

20. Maintaining Open-Mindedness

The best leaders are the ones whose minds are never closed, who are interested in hearing fresh points of view, and who are eager to deal with new issues. Even after a decision has been made, leaders should be willing to listen to contrary opinions and novel approaches. Although strong leaders do not change their minds frequently after a major decision has been made, they are not afraid to reconsider, where necessary. Those who never reconsider show a degree of rigidity and inflexibility that often spells trouble for the organization.

21. Maintaining High Standards of Dignity

When high standards of dignity are established, emphasized, and maintained, everyone can take pride in both the accomplishments and the style of the operation. The leader's role is multifaceted. By dressing well, being well mannered, avoiding profanity, helping associates through personal or family crises, conducting uplifting ceremonies, welcoming newcomers with warmly written personal letters, leaders can accomplish a great deal. A happy combination of substance and style leads to enhanced performance and high morale.

22. Giving Power Away and Making It Stick

In recent years, there has been much discussion about how to make organizations "empowering." However, empowerment does not necessarily come easy. There are three basic problem areas. Some bosses think leadership is synonymous with control and refuse to give up any power. A second type of boss sincerely tries to give power to subordinate leaders, but these subordinates do not accept it. In such cases, the associates keep giving the power back by checking with the boss, rather than taking action on their own. A third type of boss gives power away, but quickly grabs it back by micromanaging. Often without realizing it, these bosses ask too many detailed questions and check up on their associates too frequently. Leaders who truly share their power can accomplish extraordinary things. The best leaders understand that leadership is the liberation of talent; hence, they gain power not only by constantly giving it away, but also by not grabbing it back. Making empowerment stick requires much candid discussion, trust, and interaction between leaders and subordinate associates.

23. Being Generous and Magnanimous

The golden rule, "Do unto others as you would have them do unto you," is marvelous. However, in leadership situations, the platinum rule may be even better: "Treat others the way *they* would like to be treated." One of the great joys of leadership is serving associates. If a leader does not help at least five people every day, he or she probably is missing opportunities to uplift both the associates and the organization. Magnanimity, which is generosity of spirit, involves the practice of forgiveness. Some leaders have a terrible time forgiving associates who have fouled things up. Good leaders are willing to pardon those who make honest mistakes. They also pardon themselves when they make errors.

24. Nurturing the Leadership-Followership Relationship

Leadership is not synonymous with authority. It is, to a very considerable extent, a value that is entrusted to superiors by the associates. It embodies an emotional, often spiritual investment—a gift of trust. To a great extent, the associates define the conditions under which trust is given. They prescribe the qualities, characteristics, and values that the superior must possess in order to be fully accepted as the leader. It is a wise leader, indeed, who understands and nurtures this relationship between leader and followers, especially with the followers who may not be very visible. These are the fine people, doing great work, who seldom get thanked because they are "invisible." Such associates work so quietly and so competently that they often are not noticed. Without recognition and reward for their outstanding work, their morale will suffer over time. Conversely, leaders should beware of those who try to get a great deal of "face time" with the boss. These folks are often primarily concerned with serving their ambitions or their egos.

25. Welcoming Criticism and Fighting Paranoia

It is the mature leader, indeed, who accepts criticism with equanimity, calmness, and grace. Criticism can provide the very useful "reality checks" that all leaders need in order to maintain perspective. Good leaders help associates understand that it is okay to have "love quarrels" with superiors and with the organization. Associates who disagree with the leader are not the enemy. Loyalty and criticism are mutually supportive, while slavish loyalty is deadly. If an associate does something that is terribly painful to the leader, the leader should not assume that it was a deliberate act of maliciousness. A defensive crouch is not a productive response. Wise leaders never attribute to malice that which is adequately explained by stupidity.

Leaders must be brutally honest with themselves or they will slip into the terrible habit of self-deception. Even the best leaders make mistakes. By listening to criticism and quickly catching, acknowledging, and correcting mistakes, good leaders can become superb leaders.

26. Maintaining a Sense of Outrage

There are too many clever managers who work very hard to keep the boss happy and to stay out of trouble. As a result, they never allow themselves to be outraged when the system is doing serious damage to those who work for them. Instead of deflecting the heat and pressure that is flowing down from above, many managers dump all of it onto their associates. Watching bad circumstances eat away at the fabric of an organization because the leader is unwilling to challenge his or her boss can be terribly depressing to associates. A specific activity that should stimulate outrage on the part of the leader is when someone uses intimidation. Some managers allow themselves to be intimidated by their own bosses or by outsiders, and, on occasion, even by their associates. An intimidated boss can never be a great leader. The best leaders get mad on occasion and, using controlled outrage, correct the wrongs that are being levied on their people.

27. Learning from Failure

Learning from failure and bouncing back are signposts of good leadership. Bill Gates had an approach to failure that helps explain the success of Microsoft when Gates was CEO. He has been quoted as saying, "Reward worthy failure." In fact, Gates felt that if Microsoft was not failing on occasion, it must have not been pushing hard enough at the boundaries of innovation. Steve Jobs took the same approach with Apple. Too many leaders take a "zero defects" approach. They discourage risk-taking and punish those who fail. The result is often a slow "death spiral" as the organization misses out on wonderful opportunities, loses its best people, and slides downhill into mediocrity, irrelevance, or bankruptcy.

28. Building a Robust Brain Trust

One of the great success secrets of the best leaders is the building and nurturing of a brain trust. Leaders should be in close contact with two to three hundred smart and quick-thinking people outside their immediate organizations. The members of a brain trust provide wisdom and experience. Some are experts on important issues. Some are retired and often have the time to do research if they don't have the answers at their fingertips. With an active brain trust, leaders who get stuck and cannot get proper help from their immediate colleagues can find help simply by making a phone call or reaching out through email. Brain trusts offer reciprocal aid; those who participate both receive assistance and give assistance. Within your large brain trust, you should have a smaller group that serves as your ethical brain trust.

If you are confronted with an ethical dilemma and find yourself unable to sleep at night, email your friends and ask for help. If help has not arrived by the next morning, pick up the phone and ask for help.

29. Seeking and Embracing Diversity

Diversity comes in many packages, and wise leaders seek out and nourish every aspect of it. All organizations should maximize the rich diversity of opinions, heritage, cultures, races, genders, religions, personality types, and attitudes in the American culture. In fact, one of America's greatest strengths is its historic willingness to accept people of different backgrounds. However, too many leaders have a very narrow view of diversity when it comes to hiring new people. They tend to clone themselves and consider diversity only as an afterthought. The best leaders explain to their colleagues, associates, and, most importantly, to their human resource and personnel officials that they want to stress diversity in both the hiring and the promotion process.

30. Demonstrating Integrity

Leaders should not only talk about integrity but should operate at high levels of integrity. Furthermore, they should emphasize both personal and institutional integrity. Effective leaders take prompt corrective action when there are violations of integrity and upgrade the standards of institutional integrity over time. They also ensure that everybody understands their fundamental commitment to the values of the organization. Soon after assuming their leadership positions, leaders should look for ways to demonstrate such a commitment. Institutional integrity cannot lie dormant until a crisis occurs; it must be ingrained and supported by leaders at all levels. Of all the qualities that a leader must have, integrity is the most important.

Conclusion

Leadership is serving your people, serving the mission, giving power away, and raising the level of dignity and integrity in your organization. There is no human endeavor that is more fascinating, more challenging, and more rewarding than leading an organization with an important mission. Leaders who are willing to grow, learn, listen, acknowledge mistakes, teach associates, set goals, and maintain high standards are people who can help lift an organization to new heights.

SUGGESTED READING

> You are the same today that you are going to be five years
> from now except for two things: the people with whom you
> associate, and the books you read.
>
> —*Charles Jones*

The literature on leadership is rich and diverse. Having read more than five hundred books on leadership, Perry and Jeff have chosen those books that they feel provide the most useful insights and practical advice. All leaders and prospective leaders should establish and maintain a reading program. One book per month is a good goal. When you are interviewed for that job you really desire and you are asked the question, "What good books have you read lately?" if you don't have an answer, someone else will get likely get that job that you wanted so badly.

On Becoming a Leader by Warren Bennis. A preeminent authority on leadership, Bennis
   has written many books, but this one is generally considered his best. Powerful stuff.
   No bookshelf should be without it.
Great Leaders GROW: Becoming a Leader for Life by Ken Blanchard and Mark Miller.
   Lots of insights on why leaders must constantly learn and grow to be truly effective.
The Secret: What Great Leaders Know and Do by Ken Blanchard and Mark Miller. This
   is a fable that describes a great model for leadership, exposing five fundamental ways
   to become a great leader through service.
Coping with Difficult People by Robert Bramson. Dr. Bramson doesn't tell you how to fix
   difficult people. He gives you something more useful and realistic—how to cope with
   difficult bosses, peers, and associates.

Just Listen: Discover the Secret of Getting Through to Absolutely Anyone by Mark Goulston. A great book on the art of listening and enabling others to do the same.

Now, Discover Your Strengths by Marcus Buckingham and Donald Clifton. A fine book that helps you understand your talents and build them into strengths. An effective online tool is offered to assist in the discovery of your talents.

Leadership by James MacGregor Burns. This Pulitzer Prize–winning book concentrates on political leadership. Burns's discussion of transactional and transforming leadership is tremendously insightful. One caution—this book is not an easy read.

Quiet: The Power of Introverts in a World That Can't Stop Talking by Susan Cain. A fascinating analysis that helps explain why introverts often become extraordinary leaders.

How to Win Friends and Influence People by Dale Carnegie. The mega-bestseller emphasizes that leaders must have a deep, driving desire to learn, along with a vigorous determination to increase their ability to deal with people.

Integrity by Stephen L. Carter. A brilliant analysis of the most important factor in leadership.

Right from the Start by Dan Ciampa and Michael Watkins. This is the best book for those transitioning into a new leadership job.

Great by Choice: Uncertainty, Chaos, and Luck—Why Some Thrive Despite Them All by Jim Collins and Morten T. Hansen. Some fresh insights on why some corporations like Intel continue to perform at a very high standard of excellence and integrity.

7 Habits of Highly Effective People by Stephen Covey. Covey provides a holistic approach to deciphering problems and a guide to living with fairness, integrity, honesty, and human dignity.

Leadership Is an Art by Max Depree. A short, uplifting, and well-written book.

Steve Jobs by Walter Isaacson. Perhaps the most creative genius of our time, Jobs had a life story well worth reading.

If Not Now, When? by Jack Jacobs. The autobiography of an extraordinary American, Medal of Honor recipient Jack Jacobs. He brilliantly mixes humor with substance. Jacobs, who has held leadership positions in the military, in various business enterprises, and in the nonprofit sector, can serve as a fine leadership role model.

Leading Change by John P. Kotter. A bestselling book for leaders that contains a powerful eight-step process for managing change with positive results in organizations.

Endurance: Shackleton's Incredible Voyage by Alfred Lansing. A compelling book on the persistence of a leader as he overcame enormously difficult challenges in Antarctica more than one hundred years ago.

The Five Dysfunctions of a Team by Patrick Lencioni. Told in the style of a fable, this book illustrates how to build and manage a successful team based on the concept that no one makes progress, much less succeeds, alone.

5 Levels of Leadership: Proven Steps to Maximize Your Potential by John C. Maxwell. Written by a leading expert on leadership, this may be Maxwell's best book.

It Worked for Me: In Life and Leadership by Colin Powell. Lots of practical advice from an
   outstanding public servant.
Lean In: Women, Work, and the Will to Lead by Sheryl Sandberg. A brilliant analysis on
   women in leadership roles.
Leading Up: How to Lead Your Boss So You Both Win by Michael Useem. This guide will
   help your bosses be better leaders.
*The Bible on Leadership: From Moses to Matthew—Management Lessons for Contemporary
   Leaders* by Lorin Woolfe. Woolfe's book draws leadership lessons from the Bible and
   applies them to the modern world.

In addition to those books cited above we'd also recommend our
favorite authors, whose books on leaders and leadership are especially
powerful: Jim Stockdale, Forrest Pogue, Peter Drucker, Lou Holtz,
Michael Shaara, Mike Krzyzewski, Michael Howard, Martin Blu-
menson, and William Manchester.

You can gain insights on a whole range of issues relating to leadership by regularly reading three magazines we recommend highly:
BusinessWeek, the *Economist*, and the *Futurist*.

LEADERSHIP EDUCATION PROGRAMS

To every man there comes in his lifetime that special moment when he is figuratively tapped on the shoulder and offered that chance to do a very special thing, unique to him and his talents. What a tragedy if that moment finds him unprepared or unqualified for that work.

—*Winston Churchill*

We are great advocates of formal education for leaders and future leaders and are particularly taken by programs that accomplish a great deal in a fairly short time. In the following pages, we recommend a few of the very best programs that are available in the United States. Each of these programs provides opportunities for personal growth. They also allow attendees to get to know one another. The learning that occurs among the students is one of the major benefits of these programs. Anyone who is a leader, or is expecting to move into a leadership position within the next few years, and who has not already attended one of these programs should try hard to do so. It will be an invaluable experience.

The Blue Ridge Conference on Leadership is a three-day conference held each October. It attracts about five hundred leaders and potential leaders. There are four aspects of this program that are especially attractive. First, the speeches and workshops are dynamic and uplifting. Second, the cost of the conference is quite modest. Third, the setting is beautiful, peaceful, and relaxed. Fourth, there are lots of opportunities for interaction among the participants. This program is designed to help working people who already have some leadership responsibilities but aspire to move up in their companies. It attracts managers from small- and medium-sized companies throughout the South.

Blue Ridge Conference on Leadership
301 O D Smith Hall
135 South College Street
Auburn University, AL 36849
(334) 844-2870
www.blueridgeleadership.com

The Center for Creative Leadership in Greensboro, North Carolina, has a well-deserved reputation for excellence. The Center is particularly strong in the behavioral sciences; the psychological testing and evaluation program is one of the very best in the world. The CCL has a variety of programs that last from four to six days, several of which focus on creativity and innovation in organizations. Many are held at the modern and marvelously equipped facility in Greensboro, while others are held at various locations throughout the country and overseas.

Center for Creative Leadership
P.O. Box 26300
Greensboro, NC 27438-6300
(336) 545-2810
www.ccl.org

The Gallup Leadership Institute runs a five-day program at which participants learn about their own leadership talents and how they can increase levels of performance for themselves and their associates. Through the use of a structured interview, a written profile, and an individual consultation, participants discover more about their leadership strengths and how to leverage them most effectively. They develop a leadership plan to meet the specific challenges that they face. A re-measurement component allows participants to assess the impact of their leadership talents in the workplace over time.

Gallup Leadership Institute
301 South 68th Street Place
Lincoln, NE 68510
(800) 288-8592
www.gallup.com

The Ken Blanchard Companies Inc. (formerly Blanchard Training & Development) is a family-owned firm, founded by Drs. Ken and Marjorie Blanchard. Incorporated in 1979, the organization is based on three simple goals—to make a difference in people's lives, to drive human worth and effectiveness in the workplace, and to help each organization we work with become the provider, employer, and investment of choice. The company provides a host of opportunities in a variety of forums for people and organizations to learn about leadership.

Ken Blanchard Companies
125 State Place
Escondido, CA 92029
(800) 728-6000
www.kenblanchard.com

University Programs: There are a number of first-rate university leadership development programs that normally run for four or five weeks. Although they are quite expensive and demand a great deal of hard work, they are certainly worthwhile. Some of the very best include:

Columbia Senior Executive Program
Columbia Business School, Columbia University
2880 Broadway
480 Armstrong Hall
New York, NY 10025
(212) 854-6015

Program for Strategic Leadership
Smeal College of Business Administration
409 Business Administration Building
University Park, PA 16802
(814) 865-3435

Kenan-Flagler Business School for Executive Development
University of North Carolina
Rizzo Conference Center
130 DuBose Home Lane
Chapel Hill, NC 27517
(800) 862-3932

Community Leadership Programs: Numerous cities throughout the United States have excellent leadership programs. These programs serve many purposes. First, they teach leadership to people in management positions throughout the community. They are also excellent vehicles for getting bright and hardworking people together, so that they will get to know one another other well. Third, most of these programs have an alumni program, allowing people from the various year groups to interact. The programs generally run for a year. Leadership fellows usually meet once a month and take a close look at one aspect of the community—for example, the fire department, the police department, the mayor's office, a major local hospital, one or more of the local businesses.

ACKNOWLEDGMENTS

Many hundreds of people assisted in the preparation of the first edition of this book. First, the students of the National War College and the Industrial College of the Armed Forces, and the international students from the National Defense University, who took courses that Perry taught on executive leadership. These mature public servants from five military services, a dozen civilian agencies, and ten foreign nations critiqued this book in manuscript form and helped Perry refine and expand his ideas, as well as to clarify and polish the rules of thumb and the checklists.

Special thanks are due to Mary McNabb and Yvette Taylor, who took dictation by the hour and typed the manuscript; Patricia Pasquarett, who carried out many typing and editing duties; and Cathy Salvato, who accomplished many vital editorial chores. Thanks goes to Sherwood (Woody) Goldberg, who helped restructure the manuscript at a critical phase; and to Fred Kiley, Don Anderson, Walter "R" Thomas, Laura Conk, Jack Jacobs, Mike Miller, Charlie and Jane Hamm, Bob and Harriet Plowden, Ed Parks, Bill Clover, Jim Simms, Bob Sorley, Buddy Diamond, and Ken Wenker, for their valuable input and editorial comments.

A wonderful group of people gave assistance to the second and third editions. Despite their busy schedules, they spent many hours carefully reviewing the book in an effort to make the new versions much better than the first: John Barry, Norty Schwartz, Dick Chilcoat, Frank Brady, Bob Murphy, Jim Blackwell, Joe Leboeuf, Dierdre

Dixon, Lissa Young, David Haughey, John Fryer, Scott and Stacie Morgan, Fred Warren, David Kozak, Bob Elder, and Robert Fant. David Haughey deserves special thanks for reading and commenting on the text three times.

The marketing of this book gained great support when Jeff Zucker, the executive director of the *Today* show, agreed to an on-camera interview. This four-minute interview got the attention of a wide audience and the book rapidly moved up from about 23,000 on the Amazon.com list to number 2.

When a decision was made to make a major updating and revision of this book and publish it as the fourth edition, copies of the third edition were circulated among those who had used the book extensively. It was vital that outdated material be eliminated and new ideas, techniques, and concepts added. Also, the bibliography required major updating.

For this most recent edition, Perry Smith and Jeff Foley are especially appreciative of the contributions of Michael Bohn, who had been using the third edition of the book in his teaching. He recognized the need for a chapter on managing the electronic workspace and volunteered to write it. Susan Helms, the former astronaut and Air Force lieutenant general, shared her insights on managing change in large, bureaucratic organizations. Others who provided assistance include Jeff Rosensweig, Michael Ryan, Tom Clark, Vera Stewart, Thom Tuckey, John Sattler, John Stewart, Virginia Foley, Beth Foley, Connor Smith, and Ken Blanchard.

INDEX

ABOUT THE AUTHORS

Perry M. Smith is a teacher, author, and TV and radio commentator. A retired major general, Smith served for thirty years in the U.S. Air Force. During his military career he commanded an F-15 fighter wing in Germany, served as the top Air Force planner, and was commandant of the National War College. During the Vietnam War, Smith flew 180 combat missions in F-4 aircraft over Laos and North Vietnam.

Born into a military family at West Point, Smith traveled extensively throughout his youth. He watched the Japanese attack on Pearl Harbor at age six (he was on the way to Sunday school in the back of an Army truck that fateful morning). Immediately after World War II, he lived in Italy, where his father served in the British-American military government. After attending twelve schools in this country and overseas, he graduated from Highland Falls High School in New York in 1952.

General Smith graduated from the U.S. Military Academy in 1956. At West Point, he played intercollegiate lacrosse. After his senior year, he was named a member of the second all-American lacrosse team. Smith later earned his PhD in International Relations from Columbia University. His dissertation earned the Helen Dwight Reid Award from the American Political Science Association in 1968. He has written six books, including *Assignment Pentagon* and *A Hero Among Heroes: Jimmie Dyess and the 4th Marine Division*.

Smith served as CNN's military analyst from 1991 until he resigned in protest over CNN's 1998 bogus nerve gas special (*The*

Valley of Death). He later served on contract with NBC, MSNBC, CBS TV, and CBS radio.

He assisted in the editing and marketing of the book *Medal of Honor* by Peter Collier. This bestselling book profiles the remarkable life stories of our living Medal of Honor recipients.

General Smith spends much of his time teaching corporate executives, MBA scholars, government and military leaders, church groups, and nonprofits. His subjects include leadership, ethics, strategic planning, heroism, innovation, and dealing with the media. He has been an enrichment speaker for Crystal Cruises since 1992. Smith has lived in Thailand, Germany, France, Italy, and Turkey.

Since moving to Augusta in 1990, he has been active in community activities, including raising funds for the river rooms of Saint Paul's Church, the Fisher House, the Kroc Center, the Heritage Academy, and the Augusta Museum of History. Smith serves as the secretary of the Congressional Medal of Honor Foundation. He is also on the board of the Augusta Museum of History and the Augusta Warrior Project.

General Smith is married to the former Connor Cleckley Dyess. Connor is the daughter of Lieutenant Colonel Jimmie Dyess, U.S. Marine Corps—the only person to have earned America's two highest awards for heroism, the Medal of Honor and the Carnegie Medal. The Smiths have two children and five grandchildren.

Contact:
Perry M. Smith
genpsmith@aol.com
www.genpsmith.com

Jeffrey W. Foley was born and raised in Cincinnati, Ohio, graduated from the U.S. Military Academy, and retired from the U.S. Army as a brigadier general. He is an Eagle Scout and a member of

Mariemont High School Sports Hall of Fame. He participated in sports throughout college, including intercollegiate baseball at West Point.

General Foley retired from the Army in 2010 after thirty-two years of service. While in the Army, he held a variety of leadership positions in tactical signal units in Korea, Germany, and the United States. He served twice in the Pentagon and deployed to Southwest Asia in support of Operations Desert Shield and Desert Storm. He also served as the senior communications officer and chief information officer, J-6, for U.S. Central Command, MacDill Air Force Base, Florida, the command overseeing combat and peacekeeping operations in Southwest Asia, Enduring Freedom, and Iraqi Freedom.

His military career culminated in his role as the chief of the Army Signal Corps and commanding general of the Army Signal Center and School, Fort Gordon, Georgia. In this capacity, he led the development of doctrine, the strategic planning for future communications capabilities, and the professional education, training, and leader development programs for all communications and computer operations personnel in the Active, National Guard, and Reserve Army.

He has been involved in leadership development programs for his entire military career. While in the Army, he led strategic planning efforts while assigned to U.S. Central Command, Department of the Army Staff, and as the commanding general of the U.S. Army Signal Center, and since retirement he has done the same at Augusta State University and the Georgia-Carolina Council for the Boy Scouts of America. Today he is a frequently requested keynote speaker and workshop leader, speaking on becoming a leader for life, team building, personal excellence, inspiring the workforce, and strategic planning. He has spoken at state and regional conferences, university commencements, community leader development programs, other small businesses, and nonprofits. His clients have included Procter & Gamble, Bridgestone Tire Manufacturing, U.S. Army, South

Carolina Manufacturers' Alliance, Georgia Association of Chambers of Commerce, Nucor Steel, Shaw Industries, Georgia Regents University's Hull College of Business, and South East Region Rotary. He is known for his down-to-earth ability to communicate with his audiences, sharing personal experiences along with guidance from experts, ultimately inspiring in the audience a desire to listen and learn.

Since retirement from the Army, he spent two and a half years in the university system, starting at Augusta State University (ASU) as the long-range planner for campus development. Upon the consolidation of ASU and Georgia Health Sciences University, he served as Vice President of Military Affairs with the newly renamed Georgia Regents University and Health System.

He holds master's degrees in Computer Systems from the U.S. Air Force Institute of Technology, Wright Patterson AFB, Ohio, and in National Security and Strategic Studies from the National War College, Washington, DC. He is on the board of directors for Leadership Augusta, the executive board for the Georgia-Carolina Council for Boy Scouts of America, the board of directors for the Central Savannah River Area Alliance for Fort Gordon, and a national advisory board member for Lead Like Jesus, an organization cofounded by Ken Blanchard, coauthor of *The One Minute Manager.*

General Foley is married to Beth, a retired lieutenant colonel in the U.S. Army Nurse Corps.

Contact:
Jeffrey W. Foley
jwfoley@icloud.com